$\mathcal{R}$EFLECTIONS *from the* $\mathcal{O}$RIGIN

as revealed to

$\mathcal{A}myn \ \mathcal{D}ahya$

REFLECTIONS
PUBLISHING

Vancouver, Canada

Canadian Cataloguing in Publication Data
Dahya, Amyn, 1957–
Reflections from the origin

ISBN 0-9682683-1-5
1. Spiritual life. I. Title.
BL624.D33 1997   291.4   C97-910843-8

Production: Peanut Butter Publishing
Editor: Diana C. Douglas
Copy Editor: Neall Calvert
Text Design: Fiona Raven
Cover Design: David Marty
Cover Painting, *Identity*: John Pitre

First printing October 1997

10 9 8 7 6 5 4 3 2 1

REFLECTIONS PUBLISHING
18th Floor, 1500 West Georgia Street
Vancouver, BC Canada V6G 2Z6

Printed in the United States of America

EDICATION

This book is dedicated to
humanity, in the name of unity,
peace, happiness and love.

May every reader be enriched
spiritually and materially by
Reflections from the Origin.

$\mathscr{T}$ABLE OF $\mathscr{C}$ONTENTS

$\mathscr{A}$CKNOWLEDGEMENTS

Reflections from the Origin started as a dew drop of Knowledge which grew into a river and has come to us today as the Ocean of Knowledge. There are a number of people who have played an important role in this beautiful process, whose contributions I wish to acknowledge with my deepest gratitude.

I would like to start by paying a very special tribute to my wife Karima, who has been a pillar of strength in each and every moment of my life's Mission. Our children Adil, Aly, Raheena and Noorin have walked with us along a path that has not always been easy, but their love and affection have been a constant source of encouragement every step of the way.

I wish to express my deepest gratitude to my father, Sadru, mother Nabat, brother Hanif, and all members of my family, whose love and support have formed the backbone of my life, from the very first day that I can ever remember!

I wish to thank my adopted daughter, Zahra and her husband, Firdosh, my dear friend Barbara Talkington, and my cousin brother Al-Karim, for their tireless efforts in helping with the initial compilation of this book.

I would like to pay special tribute to Diana Douglas, who helped with the very difficult task of editing this book. As you can well imagine, *Reflections from the Origin* can never be "edited" by anyone, for none of us has the authority to do so, except by the Will of the Origin. Yet, the book had to be put together in a special format for publishing, and Diana's help and input was absolutely invaluable!

I extend my sincere gratitude to my dear friend John Pitre, who has produced the magnificent artwork for the cover of the book. John is truly an inspired artist, and it is only fitting that his work be used for the very first impression of *Reflections from the Origin*.

I would also like to acknowledge with sincere appreciation, the support of my special friends Edmund de Rothschild, C.B.E. and his wife Anne, for their review of the manuscript.

I thank all the members of the Peanut Butter Publishing team: Elliott Wolf, publisher; Diana Douglas, managing editor; Jake Jennings, text input; Fiona Raven, text designer; Neall Calvert, copy editor; and David Marty, cover designer.

As each day goes by, there will be more and more people who will participate in the wonderful blessing of *Reflections from the Origin*. There will be those who will help with the marketing, promotion and distribution of the book throughout the globe. Then, there will be those who will read this book and encourage their friends and relatives to participate in this blessing. There will be those who will teach their children and loved ones about the Principles of Living learned from this book. To all of you, my beloved friends, I extend my sincere gratitude and pray that you be enriched by *Reflections from the Origin* forever.

$\mathcal{M}$ESSAGE TO THE $\mathcal{R}$EADER

Today marks a very special day in my life, for by delivering this book to you, I have fulfilled a very important Mission that was entrusted to me by the Origin, the Source of all Creation.

It all began in 1993, when I found myself waking up in the middle of the night and writing feverishly without knowing what I was actually writing. I found myself rising into a state of peace and spiritual elevation as I watched my pen move at the speed of light! At first I did not know what to do or how to react to this wonderful experience. Each time I read what I had written, I was dumbfounded with the depth of the Knowledge that had flowed through me. I shared these writings with my wife and very close members of my family, for, by and large, I considered this experience to be a very private matter. However, it was clear to me that a very special process had begun, whose roots extended far beyond the material world.

As time went by, I began to experience the Light, and the Revelations became more intense and powerful. I found myself "hearing" the Voice of the Origin as I swiftly recorded the Knowledge that flowed through me. It was a truly humbling experience; I felt like a speck of dust that was being addressed by the Universe!

I was then commanded to deliver this Knowledge to all my fellow human beings, at each and every corner of the Earth. It was clear to me that my role was simply to be a Messenger who was guided to deliver a personal Message, from the Origin, to each and every reader. I was told that each Chapter in this book would carry a very special and personal meaning to the reader. No two people would have exactly the same interpretation of what has been written, because the Message will strike a very personal chord in the heart and Soul of the reader. After all, *Reflections from the Origin* is a direct communication between you and the Origin. I am simply a humble Servant, through whose privileged hand this Message has come (to you). If only I could tell you how great a responsibility it has been for me to carry what is truly a gift to humanity from the Origin! Now, this part of my task is complete and I am truly grateful for that. However, there is still a lot left for me to do, because I could not fit all the Revelations that I have received to date in one book! Therefore, there will be further volumes.

When you read this book, I recommend that you pause at the end of each Chapter to Reflect upon the Message. Take the time to read each Chapter over and over again and meditate upon what is being said. Each time you read a Chapter again, you will discover a new meaning! This book is not to be read like a novel, because there is a great deal that you can learn from it. It is very important to Reflect upon what you read. You will often find that the burning questions that you have carried with you since childhood may be answered as you read this book. If you are at a crucial decision-making point in your life, you will find guidance that will help you make these decisions. If you are in a relationship that you are questioning or wondering about, there will be that one special Chapter that will clarify things for you. My dear friends, *Reflections from the Origin* is your book on Living. It has answers and advice for you that will impact all facets of your life.

Throughout the course of human history, the Origin has sent Messengers with Knowledge to be shared with humanity. Sometimes this Knowledge took the form of new religions. However, in this day and age, there is no need for a new religion. Instead, it is most important for us to stop and think about ourselves and our lives. We need to search for the Essence of whatever faith we believe in, because, as you will learn from this book, there is truly no difference between the fundamental Essence and Principles of today's religions. *Reflections from the Origin* has Messages for people of all religions, cultures and walks of life, including those who do not believe in the concept of God at all!

As you read this book, you will notice that certain key Chapters have been grouped together. For example, there are seven Chapters entitled "Message to the Scientist" (Chapters 31 to 38); these reveal scientific principles that will be the norm one hundred years from today. Scientists who follow the principles revealed in these Chapters will make breakthroughs and discoveries of an unprecedented nature!

Chapter 46, entitled *The 66 Steps: My Ascension to the Light*, represents the climax of this book, where the journey of the Soul was revealed to me through a vision of my ascension of an old staircase in Jerusalem. This beautiful Chapter paves the way for the reader to recognize the impact of this lifetime on the timeless journey of the Soul. This will lead to the desire to embark on an Inner Search for Enlightenment.

Towards the end of the book is a group of seven Chapters entitled "In Search of the Light" (Chapters 39 to 45). These Chapters describe the Light of the Origin and offer guidance (to those who are ready and interested) on the process of searching for this Light. Once again, these Chapters must be read repeatedly for you to derive full benefits from them. When you are ready to practise daily meditation, these Chapters will provide invaluable guidance that will help in the Search for the Light. What better teacher can one ask for than the Origin!

The book concludes with a letter from me to my four children, Adil, Aly, Raheena and Noorin. This letter describes my life and carries special advice that every parent can share with his or her child. The perspectives it contains could help shape children's lives for a successful and meaningful tomorrow.

My dear friends, it is time for us to take a break from our busy material lives and think about why we are here, and what is the purpose of our lives. I was once asked by a friend how I could measure the value of my life. To this I replied that he and I would both have to look at the world two hundred years from now. The Mercedes-Benz that I love will probably have been recycled five times, and part of it would even have ended up as a teaspoon on a restaurant table! The house that he loves so dearly will probably be occupied by the fifth generation of strangers who would not even recognize him if he showed up at the doorstep! Hence, our beautiful cars, homes and material possessions, which we value so greatly today, would probably be completely insignificant two hundred years from now!

However, if some of us were teachers or doctors who practised their profession with sincerity, we could say that we made a permanent impact on the lives of numerous generations. Alternatively, if we were scientists or businessmen who had brought safe water supply to a disease-stricken area, we may see a thriving community two hundred years from now, and have the satisfaction of knowing that we had played a part. If we dispose of our wastes carefully today, we may have gardens instead of polluted landfill sites two hundred years from now. As a matter of fact, my dear friends, at this stage in my life, I seldom enter into activities, projects or business deals that do not meet my Two-Hundred-Year Test!

By sharing this simple example with you, I am trying to suggest that we develop an outlook that will add meaning to our lives. Since *Reflections from the Origin* is our book on Living, let's start the process from here!

I hope and pray that this book may enrich your life as it has mine. Writing this book has been the greatest learning experience for me; I have gained Knowledge that could seldom be found in any academic institution. Since I can claim no ownership of these Pearls of Wisdom, I have undertaken to donate 100% of the profits from the sale of this book to the Bismillah Children's Foundation, a non-profit institution that is helping and serving the needs of underprivileged children throughout the world.

My dear friends, the Knowledge in this book is all yours as a gift from the Origin!

THE *S*TATEMENT OF *U*NIVERSAL *T*RUTH

The Origin is the Creator of All Things (the Universe).

The Origin created human beings, from the outer shell to the mind, intellect and self.

The Origin bestowed humanity with all that is needed to survive in this world, which is part of Creation.

The Origin has bestowed humanity with the freedom to choose and the flexibility to think, imagine and plan for its future.

The journey of life is a multitude of crossroads. At each crossroad we choose our direction, and this choice forms the basis for the next crossroad.

The Origin provides guidance at all times, at each and every crossroad. Those that seek this guidance are blessed with the inspirations to make the correct choices. Those that do not seek this guidance continue down their own paths to a destiny unknown.

The Origin has bestowed upon humanity a fundamental guiding principle, which is the Statement of Universal truth, that says:

"*Each one of us is a part of the Creator.
Therefore, I am You and You are Me.
Together We are Everything.*"

The Origin has revealed to humanity the Statement of Universal Truth in many different ways throughout history. For example, the Ten Commandments as revealed through Moses (Peace be upon Him), have their origins in this special Statement. However, the Ten Commandments were broken down into a specific form that could be understood and adhered to by the people of that time, in accordance with their level of intellectual development and consciousness.

The Origin has revealed the Statement of Universal Truth to humanity today in its purest and most fundamental form, so that we may understand, digest, internalize and apply it in each and every decision that we make in our lives.

ONE

THE *Gotthard Tunnel*

On May 4, 1993, I drove with my friends Sandro and Beat from Stanstaad to Lugano in Switzerland to visit with Werner Krupp, the famous natural scientist. The drive took us through the Alps and the view was spectacular. The setting was "perfect." There were snow-capped peaks, green peaks, luscious green valleys with emerald green lakes, and crystal-clear rivers. The land had a vibrant sense of peace.

The Gotthard tunnel is the longest tunnel in the world — sixteen kilometres, with no breaks in between. It goes through the belly of the Alps. As we approached it, we closed off all vents in the car to keep out the polluted air and exhaust fumes. When the car entered the tunnel, we were greeted with darkness. As I looked back, I could see the beautiful sunlight disappear. The tunnel gave me a sense of loneliness. The lights were dim and the distance ahead seemed too long and cumbersome. I could not look forward to anything but the rapid passage of time.

After a few minutes, I began to grow accustomed to the darkness. It didn't feel so bad. I looked at the oncoming vehicles and the trucks in front of us. I noted all the S.O.S. telephone booths and Emergency Exits. Once I had forgotten the sunshine, trees, rivers and valleys, the tunnel seemed to be okay. Life in the darkness began to seem normal. Each time I looked at an Emergency Exit, I thought about the "outside." It felt precious! But then again, as soon as I focused back into the tunnel, the "outside" became a remote concept in the back of my mind. The question often popped up into my mind, how much longer to go? I wondered what it would be like if the tunnel suddenly caved in. It would be okay, since the only thing that would remain would be the "outside." I watched the signs counting down the kilometres to the end of the tunnel. By this time, we were about midway. The car began to feel uncomfortable and stuffy. Despite the closed vents, I could smell fumes.

The car had no air-conditioning, or else it would not have been so bad. I felt like opening my window — but then it would only get worse. My mind then drifted off onto the subject of business. I became somewhat oblivious to the dark, narrow, lonely and polluted tunnel. I conceptualized our diamond mines in South Africa. I thought about how that deal could be financially connected to the well-being and growth of our environmental company. We have a lot of work to do in this world, I thought aloud. Will I have enough time to do it all? Just then, I saw the "1 km" sign. Soon we would be out of the tunnel.

My mind shifted back to the tunnel. It was still the same — a dark, hollow mess! Then, in the distance, I could see a bright speck of light. As we drew closer, the walls of the tunnel began to be illuminated. The light grew bigger and bigger — and then there was a "snap"! We were out, back into the sunshine, with the trees, mountains, rivers and lakes. It felt wonderful. I felt a strong sense of inner satisfaction and peace. I immediately opened my window and took in a deep breath of fresh air. The rays of this beautiful warm Sun penetrated their way right into my Soul. I looked back at the tunnel as it disappeared into the distance. That is when the coin dropped! I realized that I had just experienced *birth, life* and *death*!

Before I was born, I soared freely through the skies; the Beloved with the Lover. I could go wherever I wanted to go, be whatever I wanted to be, feel whatever I wanted to feel … I was "Me." And, in the Divine Light of the Origin, I was "Light." I was warm, comfortable, peaceful, happy and loved. I had no limits, I was Infinite.

Then came my time to separate from my Origin, like a spark separates itself from the fire. The Origin came to bid me farewell, and to tell me of my Mission that lay ahead. I was engulfed by the Divine Love and then there was a painful parting as I broke away. The Origin would always be with me throughout my Mission. I was never to forget that.

Then, I was encaged in the womb of my mother, in this little shell called the human body. The encagement and parting from the Origin was like entering the tunnel. As I looked back, I could see the Light bidding me farewell. Then It disappeared and I was born....

At the beginning, I was very uncomfortable being in this helpless little shell. I longed to break out and run back to the Light — but it was too late. It was hard — very, very hard. But, the Origin was always with me, and the Divine Love made me feel at ease, as I struggled through the new experience of loneliness and imprisonment. How long was my sentence to be? I knew I had a job to do and I pondered how it was going to be done. The Origin was always with me and this Knowledge made it easier for me to accept the loss of my freedom.

I began to get used to this shell, just as I got accustomed to the dark Gotthard tunnel. The less I thought of the Light, the more comfortable I got within the tunnel. In fact, I began to enjoy the tunnel! Ninety-nine percent of my abilities were severed through this encagement — yet, I enjoyed the meagre one percent! I had a father, mother and a brother. Life was fun and I was all engrossed with life! I also forgot about my real Origin, my real Home, and the real Me. The dim lights of the polluted tunnel seemed okay to me. By this time, I was a young adult — full of life

and lots to look forward to in my one-percent realm! I
learned about God, but I could not remember the
Light any more. The notion of the Origin had now
become what we call Faith! Believing, but not seeing.
"Have faith," I was told by my parents and teachers.
How can you "need" faith in the "Knowledge of the
Certain"? I pondered. My simple human mind could
not comprehend this. I even identified myself as
Amyn — the one that I saw in the mirror — the shell!
The real Me is so much larger — as large as the Ocean.
But, all I could see was the droplet — a microfraction
of the real Me. And, believe it or not, I was actually
proud of what I saw in the mirror! How naive!

Then, I saw the Emergency Exit sign in the tunnel.
The symbol showed a man running up the stairs to the
"outside." He had a way of breaking out of the tunnel
and into the warm, clear, beautiful "outside." The sign
brought back memories of my freedom, but then they
quickly passed. I was comfortable with the tunnel
again. I got so involved with my business, my wife, my
children and all that was around me, that I forgot
about the tunnel itself, let alone that there was an
"outside"!

But now, I am back in the tunnel and I see the
countdown of kilometres to its end. Have I
accomplished my Mission? Oh! But what is my
Mission? I cannot remember! Why did I put up with
such a severe encagement in a closed shell that is
rapidly ageing?! There must be a reason for paying this
price! But what is the reason? I try hard to think, but

my mind is limited to the capacity of the shell. I try hard to remember, but it is of no use. Then, I realize that I am using the wrong avenue to "remember."

The Knowledge is within Me, the ninety-nine percent and not the shell — the one percent! The Origin is with Me, as always. So, I must seek the Knowledge from within myself. Through the Love and Mercy of the Origin, I have been put onto the course of my Mission without even knowing it! Just as I am the Beloved of the Divine Light, so are all other Souls around — for they too are from the Origin. My Mission involves doing Good — for all the Beloved Souls; for all Creation. I never even realized that I have been bestowed with all the tools that I need. I have been blessed with the education, the intellect, the personality, the openings to business and thus "transport" of wealth, the ability to love and forgive (I try, at least!), and above all, the Closeness to the Origin. So, I am on my way to accomplishing my Mission. I must do my very best, and leave the outcome of my efforts in the hands of the Origin.

Then, I see another one kilometre go by on the countdown. I ask myself, will I have enough time to do what I have to do? Of course, when the Origin leads the way, I will accomplish.... Then, I see another Emergency Exit sign. I ask myself, why can't I break out and go to the outside — take a deep breath of fresh air, and then come back into the tunnel to complete my Mission? Of course, I can! But it must be, and can only be, by the Divine Will. So, I will keep on trying....

I know that the last 1km sign will come soon, bringing me closer to the Light. Then, the walls of the tunnel will start to illuminate. And then, the Light at the end of the tunnel will grow. Suddenly, I will break out. Free again! Warm at last! Engulfed by the Divine Love, comfortable and happy. I will look back at the tunnel and wave goodbye to the loved ones that I will have left behind. I hope and pray that my Mission will be complete and that I will have won the happiness of my Creator — for I never want to go into that tunnel again!

Through this little understanding that I have been blessed with, I pray that the walls of the tunnel be illuminated for me now and throughout my Mission — not just before the end, for then it may be too late. I pray that I may always be close to the Origin, just as I was before I entered the tunnel. I pray that I may be guided by the Divine Light throughout my Mission. I came into the tunnel with nothing. There is little in this place that is of value for me to keep. For, when I break out of it, I will leave all my material possessions behind and will take nothing with me. All that I came with was my Mission. I pray that I may leave with this Mission fully accomplished to the satisfaction of my Creator.

One thing I have recognized for sure, is that it is a lot more difficult to be born than it is to die!

When I look around me, there is so much hate, anger, evil and greed. It is all manifested in people. Yet, behind each of these "shells" is a wonderful, dignified Soul that is as large as the Ocean. However, the droplets govern in the tunnel!

I pray that we may all be able to see and fulfil our Mission. May we be blessed with Light, so that the walls of our tunnel may be illuminated before it is too late. May we experience no more pain, sorrow, hate, greed and evil. May there be only "Good," everywhere. And, may the "Good" overflow and cover forever the evil, just like the Ocean covers the land that lies beneath it. This can Be — for when the Origin says Be — It Is!

Received on May 4, 1993.

TWO

THE *R*OSE

I was on a flight from Frankfurt to Los Angeles.
After the plane took off, I was offered a Rose by the
air hostess. It was beautiful and smelt pleasant. I felt
sorry for it. I said to the Rose, "The Origin has blessed
you with beauty and scent. This blessing has led you
to your death! For that, I am sorry."

But the Rose replied, *"My purpose on earth is to
show beauty to humanity — to provide all with
the fragrance of Love. I am a symbol of Love. That
is why I am offered by the Lover to the Beloved.
The prettier I am, and the more beautiful I smell,
the stronger will be My message to humanity. So,
do not be sorry for Me, Amyn, for I have fulfilled
My purpose — this should make you happy for
both of us! You, too, are like a rose to your Origin.
So, when your mission is fulfilled, you too will be*

plucked from the garden, to be with the Origin for Eternity. That is what Life is all about."

By the end of the flight, my dear Rose had wilted. That is the second message she had to give to me. *"We will all wilt one day. Death will come to us all. Complete your mission, and seek Union with the Origin before you wilt. For then, you will remain Eternally Fresh from Within. Around you, there are many reminders and signals. Do not be blind to them! By the way, did you notice my thorns? This tells you that Life and Love can be beautiful, but not always easy. There are thorns that will hurt you, as they have hurt the greatest of people that have come before you. The Origin is your Healer. Become One with the Origin and each thorn will become to you a Rose in itself. Farewell, my dear. I have delivered to you the three messages that I was sent to you for."*

Received on October 30, 1993.

THREE

THE *M*IRAGE

It was early morning. The Sun had begun to rise. I had been running around in the forest for days, not knowing where I was going. Each time I reached what looked like a path, there were at least four directions I could take. I often looked to the sky, for the Sun to guide me. But the forest was so dense that I could not see the Sun. I knew that it was daytime, but very often the Sun just seemed to be like a distant haze over the leaves of the trees. I did not know how long I had been wandering in this forest. I was desperate to get out of it. I would have given anything for a drink of cool, fresh water. I could not recount the number of crossroads that I had encountered in the forest; all I knew was that there were many. And, for all I knew, I could have been travelling in circles for days! Maybe I was where I had started. Or maybe I was a long ways away! I wished that someone would show up to guide me. But, from where? And, in such a dense forest, with no distinct landmarks, how could anyone find their way?

Just then, I looked at the ground and the soil started to appear to be white in colour. My heart beat with excitement! Then I heard the flow of water — there was a river close by! I yearned for this beautiful sound of flowing water. I would have given anything for it! And then, the sound got closer as I came to a clearing in the forest. The soil was now completely white and I looked at this beautiful river, whose crystal-clear water glittered in the morning Sun. It was like a golden serpent. The water frolicked over the rocks playfully, inviting me to rush to it and drink to my heart's content. I ran towards the water and threw my hands out to scoop up this precious blessing. My thirst had reached an unbearable level. But then, suddenly, I found myself thrusting my hands into hot burning sand! All I scooped out to rinse my face with was hot burning sand! What had happened? Where was the cool water that I had so dearly desired? Where was the river? Where were the frolicking ripples? I felt cheated. I felt angry. I felt a rage that could have made me destroy everything around me. Even if a guide had shown up now, I could have killed him or her.

I ran around screaming and pounding my feet on the burning sand. I looked into the sky and saw the Sun shining down on me for the first time in days. I could have cared less! I had forgotten the misery I had felt in the forest when I could not find the Sun. It was now here, but I felt completely indifferent. A few moments ago I would have given anything to find the Sun, for then I could be guided by its position in the sky. And, I could have enjoyed its warm rays that would bring life and warmth to my cold, damp, weary cheeks.

I cried out to the Origin: "How cruel can You be? After showing me the river and raising all my hopes, You took it away! How cruel can You get? They all said that You were Merciful. That is not true! In the name of the Heavens, it is not true!" I sat in the sand and wept.

Then I heard a loud, clear and powerful Voice say to me, *"I am not the One that is cruel. There never was a river; it was a mirage that you had created in your mind. It was something that you had wanted so dearly that, behold, by the power of intellect that I have given to you, you created the illusion of a river! It was only a mirage. Had I willed that the river be there, I would simply say, 'Be,' and it would Be. But, my dear one, your anger and disappointment are nothing but your own folly.*

"When you desire something so much, you force everything around you to fit your desires. You must learn to 'Let it Be'. Do not force the events and the circumstances to meet your desires. That will make you unhappy, as you are now. Look at yourself, you look miserable! Learn to let your

desires follow the events and not the reverse. Had
you done so, you would now be very happy, for
after days of wandering, I have led you to the Sun!
A drink of cool water could never have led you out
of this forest which you found so miserable. But
the Sun would have! Learn to recognize the signs
that I have placed around you to see and follow.
Some things in life bring short- term, immediate
gratification, like the sip of the cool river water that
you had so desired. Yet, you really were not going
to die without water because the leaves of the
forest that fed you gave you all the water that you
needed. Yet, look at you, how angry and hurt you
are. What you really needed was the clearing in
the forest from where the Sun and Stars could
guide you back to your home. I knew better what
you needed. Yet now that you have received what
you so desperately needed, you do not recognize
it with gratitude! Rather, you call Me cruel for what
you did not find! The reason you could not find the
river was that it never existed; you chased a
mirage!

"My dear one, learn to count the blessings that
you have, for they are really yours. And, do not
grieve for what you do not have for they are not
yours. Do not mould all your circumstances and
events to fit your desires, for more often than not,
all you will find is a mirage. Yet, if you place your
trust in Me, and follow the path that I lead you
upon, you will find that your desires will follow the

events, and you will find what is truly important, like the Sun that you just found. Live your life in this way and the anger, pain and grief that you feel right now will touch you no more! Celebrate this day, for you have been guided and shown a way out of this forest! And remember, tomorrow there will be another forest...."

Received on February 2, 1995.

The above beautiful parable tells us all about Life. Let us learn from it, my dear friends.

Let us sit back in a quiet room and list all the things in our lives today that make us happy. Let us list all the things that we would never trade for anything.

Then, let us list all the things that we have a burning desire to get.

By doing this simple exercise we will realize that the Sun has shone upon us. We just did not know it! And from all our burning desires, we will see mirages that we must guard against. I am not saying that there must be no desires. All I am saying is let us guard against the mirages. Let us place our trust in the Origin so that we may find happiness....

FOUR

ESSENCE

The Voice of Inspiration says:

"No two things can be more 'equal' than you and your fellow being. Yet, no two things can be more 'different' than you and your fellow being."

In Nature, no two things are "ever" the same. Even no two cells in your very own body are the same. You cannot get any closer. Yet, everything in Nature has the "Same Essence." It is only the Form that is different. Isn't it wonderful how something so different can be so much the same — in fact Equal?

Received on May 7, 1993.

FIVE

$\mathcal{M}$OTHER $\mathcal{W}$ATER:
HER MESSAGE TO THE WORLD

On a trip to the heart of the Swiss Alps I visited a beautiful lake. As I looked at the precious, crystal-clear Water, I knew I needed to open up to Her, and learn from Her. We began a conversation — a beautiful conversation with no words. I am honoured to share this wonderful conversation with you.

I asked the Water, "In what language must I communicate with you?"

She said, *"I understand all languages — of humans, birds, animals, plants, everything. I form a major part of you and all living things. Hence, I know* all *about* all *living things — for they are Me. So Amyn, language is not a question! I have the deepest Knowledge of everything within Me — for I am the common element in everything. Look to Me and I will share this Knowledge with you, for you will understand."*

She then said, *"I am your Mother, I am the Mother of all. Even in the womb of your mother, I was the sea (amniotic sea) that sheltered you, protected you and fed you. I did not let the largest of bumps hurt you, whilst I tenderly cared for you in the womb. Even your very first feed from your mother's breast was Me. I am your Mother. Look around you. Everything you see is Me. Do you find the trees beautiful? Well, what is the tree? Water, of course! How does the tree make food? Through Me! Hence, I feed you and even every breath you take is Me (water vapour in the air). Look at the sea! I am the home for all creatures of the sea. I am the Provider and I am a major part of everything that lives on land. If you want to understand the true meaning of the word Giving — look at Me. I am available to all — rich, poor, animal, bird, plant.... When you need Me, you can drink Me. Whatever your need — air, food, shelter — it all comes from Me. I give without question. I expect nothing in return. I am all-giving. Generosity is a quality of our Origin. Look at Me and you will know what it means!*

"I am your Mother. I give you all and ask for nothing in return but your Love and Respect. The human race has used Me. For their greed and

gain they have used Me, polluted Me, and hurt My purity. Stop all from hurting Me — from polluting Me. I will give and will always give — for I am your Mother. Amyn, you want to remove pollution from Me. You want to purify Me so that I can bless all My children with good health. I have all the Knowledge in Me — look to Me and I will share it with you. Use it correctly and you will achieve your Mission.

"For those that do not understand Me, I am water, just water — to drink, use, wash your car and dump your waste! I am Life, I am your Mother. Love Me and care for Me, for I am all yours. I am all-giving. Remember, I am your Mother and you are Me. Love Me, Respect Me and Look to Me.

"Amyn, you have often wondered about why water is poured as the last rite over the grave of the deceased. For those who can see, it is a universal acknowledgement that Life begins with Me and ends with Me."

Received on July 2, 1993.

My dear friends, think about this wonderful message that we have received from Mother Water. Think about how She Loves and Cares for us. What can we do for Her in return?

SIX

THE *S*PARROW AND THE *D*OVE

Many a time, I have listened to conversations where
people of different professions, races and interests
have discussed God. In some cases, the tone of the
conversation is calm and peaceful. In other cases, there
are heated debates. Some challenge those that believe
in God. Others argue about the very existence of God.
Some with strong views ridicule others, condemning
them for their difference in beliefs, and so it goes on
and on…. It is a debate. It is emotional, funny, fearful,
scornful, sad, rational and irrational! What a debate!
Who is right, and who is wrong? This is typically the
issue. I wonder, why does anyone have to be right? Or,
why does anyone have to be wrong? And, who is to
decide between right and wrong? Are we capable of

making such a judgement? If so, on what basis, one must ask. This is another debate!

There was once a sparrow that flew in the sky. It looked at the earth and only saw green fields. Then, it flew over a lake, and the earth was one solid mass of water in the eyes of this sparrow. Then, it flew over a mountain covered with snow; the world now seemed to be a sheet of plain white! Then, the sparrow flew over the desert and saw the earth as one mass of brown sand! As it flew on its journey, it saw trees, grass, water, snow, rocks, sand, rich green fields and dry brown deserts. Then, it landed on a tall baobab tree to rest. One half of the baobab tree had leaves and the other half had none! Just then, a white dove landed on the baobab tree, also to rest.

The two birds looked at each other and the sparrow asked, "Where are you headed to?"

The dove replied, "My entire life is a journey, with a destination I know not."

The sparrow then asked, "Where do you live? Above what part of the land is your home?"

The dove replied, "The land is the earth and the earth is the land — I can tell no difference."

"But," said the sparrow, "I live above the land with the rich green grass — that is my home, and that is the *only* earth there is."

The dove then asked, "Have you ever flown over the glittering land which shines in the Sunshine and looks deep and lonely in the darkness? And when the wind blows, this land has ripples and waves — sometimes it rages with waves and splashes all over?"

The sparrow replied, "Of course I have flown over that glittering land, but that is *not* the earth! And, I once tried to step on it, but the land was false. I could not set my feet on this glittering land, because each time I tried, the land opened up and in went my feet! My dear dove, that is a false land, and it is not the earth for sure!"

The dove then asked, "Have you ever flown over the brown sands that blaze in the heat?"

The sparrow had a frown on its face. "Of course, I have seen those strange lands. Each time I set foot on the brown land, I jumped up because my feet kept getting burnt. Like the false land that parted each time I set foot on it, these sands too are false because all they do is burn my feet! And, I can assure you, these sands are *not* the earth!"

Then said the dove, "You must have flown over the land that almost touches the sky?"

The sparrow had a smile on its face. "Yes, but that land too is false because when I look at it from afar, it is touching the sky. But, when I fly over it, the sky is a long, long ways away! Once I tried to set foot on the white fluff (snow) that grows on top of this land, and it felt very strange! I felt the same pain as I did when I tried to stand on the brown sand. But, whilst the pain felt the same, it was still different. I think this land never tells the truth. It looks different to me every time I look at it, from afar and from close by. That could never be the home for anybody; that could *never* be the earth!"

By this time, the dove was quite amused. The sparrow seemed to have seen the different lands, but only *its* home was the earth! Everything else was false or strange! The dove then asked the sparrow, "What if I were to say that all the lands that you saw are the earth?"

The sparrow replied, "With due respect, my dear dove, I would have to say that you are mad — only a mad bird could say something so absurd! There is only one earth, and that is where the rich green grass grows. Everything else is false!"

The dove then said, "All the lands we talked about — the glittering land, the burning sands, the white fluff — are they not all 'lands', for that is what you have called them all along?"

"Yes," replied the sparrow. "But they are all very different and so they are false!"

The dove then said, "My dear sparrow, you agree that all these false places are 'lands', but since they behave strangely to you, you cannot understand them. But, they are all 'lands'. Suppose I were to say that they are one 'land' with differences?"

The sparrow seemed to get very flustered. "You cannot have all these strange 'lands' in one 'land'! The only land that I think is real is the green land where I live, and that, my dear friend, is the 'earth.' I know this for sure because I live there. It is as real as real can be, and everything else is false!"

The dove could see that although the sparrow had seen much, it understood little. Here was a bird that had travelled far and wide, and seen lands that were so different; yet, the green field was the only reality it knew. The dove, being a wise bird, asked the sparrow, "Would you say that we are both standing on a baobab tree?"

To that the sparrow replied, "Of course. We are here, aren't we?"

The dove then said, "Would you say that this tree has leaves?"

The sparrow replied, "Of course. Are you blind?"

The dove flapped its wings and said, "Look behind you. Do you see any leaves on that half of the tree?"

The sparrow replied, "No, there are no leaves on that part of the tree, but it is a baobab tree. I know because I am standing on it!"

The dove smiled and said, "So you agree that it is a tree that we are standing on?"

"Of course!" replied the sparrow.

"But one half of the tree is so different from the other. So, why don't we say that this tree is in fact two different 'trees'?"

The sparrow looked confused and said, "You have a point, but this is one tree, I can assure you!"

"Well, if this is so, why can't the 'lands' be one 'land'? And this one 'land' be the 'earth'?"

The sparrow had a twinkle in its eye. It said, "I guess you have a point. You may have sold me on the 'tree' story, but the 'earth' is a whole different matter. *I guess you doves really need to be sparrows to know what the 'earth' is!*"

My dear friends, in every debate about God, there are sparrows and doves. The very idea that God exists is difficult for some to understand. And then, there are others who think that their religion and perception of God is the only "true path" — just like the sparrow and the green field. Then, there are some that view God through the physical things that surround them. There are others who view God in a spiritual context. Some atheists or those who do not understand God, say that what we call "God" is just a form of "Energy"

or a form of "Statistical Coincidence." We all describe God in so many different ways.

But the truth is that everything boils down to one common Origin. All the rays of this great disarray we call life focus sharply on an "Origin." You may call that Origin whatever you please. I refer to the Origin as "God," or "Allah." Think of the sparrow and the dove — two birds talking about different lands that had been seen and felt by both, but interpreted completely differently. The sparrow in its own right was correct in what it saw and felt. But then, so was the dove. Yet, my dear friends, all they talked about were the desert sands, green fields, snow-capped mountains, and lakes. But when, to their concept of "earth," you start to add the deep blue oceans, the skies, stars, planets and the entire Universe, it starts to become very, very complex. Could you imagine the debate between the sparrow and the dove on this expanded definition of "earth"?

My dear friends, when we think of God — that very thought alone is wonderful. And when we talk about our beliefs or opinions, we must remember the sparrow and the dove, for there is no wrong and no right! Why should anyone be "wrong" in their perception of God? And then, why should anyone be "right" about God? Who can judge between the right and the wrong? God only knows…!

If anyone should ever suggest that their view of God is the only correct one, and that everything else is false, then they may have been spending too much time with the sparrow! You may want to suggest the broader perspective of the dove. But even that may be nowhere near broad enough!

Received on June 30, 1994.

In our search for the Truth, I pray that we may be blessed with a perspective that is not even limited by the size and extent of the infinite Universe. May we constantly seek the truth, for it is by the will of the Origin that we will discover the Ultimate Truth.

THE $\mathscr{C}$ACTUS AND THE $\mathscr{P}$RINCE

There was once a cactus tree that grew in the hot, blazing sands of the Kalahari Desert. This poor tree, having no neighbours, lived a solitary life. It must have been at least one hundred years old. Its base was dry and woody but as one looked higher, its colour turned to shades of luscious green. It must have had at least one hundred leaves. From each leaf emerged at least ten thorns. On some leaves, delicate bright pink flowers grew and developed into fruit with fine, but sharp, hair that could chase away any unwelcome intruders.

Then, one morning as the Sun rose, the cactus looked towards the horizon and saw a man, dressed in a white robe, approaching on the back of a tall, healthy, majestic camel. The poor lonely cactus tree was filled with joy, for after a long time a visitor had cared to come by. Slowly and surely, the camel walked along in the hot desert sand and came closer to the anxiously waiting tree. Then, when it was finally there, the rider stopped and got off the back of his camel. He walked over to the cactus with long, firm and authoritative strides.

The cactus called out to him and said, "May the Peace of the Origin be upon you, O Visitor. I have waited so long for you to come by."

The Visitor replied, "I am the Prince of the Desert. I rule the entire kingdom that covers these sands from the north to the south, and from the east to the west. Everything that lives on this land, which is my kingdom, is my property! Therefore, O sorry tree, bow down before your Majesty for your life and death rests in these mighty hands."

Having waited for so long to be visited by anyone, the poor cactus was filled with dismay. The arrogant Prince brought neither love nor peace to be shared with the creatures of the desert! The cactus calmly replied, "O Prince of the Desert, I am delighted to be honoured by the presence of your Majesty. I am willing, in the name of the Origin, to offer to you whatever you please, just as I have offered to all the beloved travellers that have gone by. My leaves are filled with precious, precious water that can quench your thirst, O Prince of the Desert. My flowers bear the sweetest-tasting fruits that I welcome you to savour. My leaves cannot offer the shade that the trees of the forest can, but, if you care to rest in my shadow, I will protect your skin from the blazing Sun. And, if all you want is a prayer for your good fortune, then in the name of the Origin, I will offer my humblest prayers to the Creator of All, that you may receive fulfilment of all your good wishes."

The Prince drew his sharp, shining silver sword and placed its cold blade against the stem of the poor cactus. "You did not hear me, O miserable creature of solitude! I commanded you to bow to me, for I am your Prince. Your life is my property! If you care to look, with one single blow, I could put an end to your life! I do not care to receive your leaves, or your water, or your fruits, or shade or prayers! These are offerings that are received by poorer men and those of lesser stature than me! I am the Prince of the Desert! I have the purest water in my gourd that has been cooled by the fanning of my slaves throughout the night! Why should I bother with chewing your miserable leaves?! I have feasted on fruits that come from every corner of the earth. Anything that is less than perfect is not even eaten by my slaves, lest they may not be able to serve me with their utmost vigil! Why on earth would I bother to eat your fruit that is covered with hairs, thorns and dust? That would indeed be an insult to my palate, for which you would have to pay with your life! And as for your prayers, O thorny creature of solitude, I do not need anyone to pray for the fulfilment of my good wishes or for the receipt of my good fortune. I have it all, and what I don't have, I take from whomsoever and wheresoever I choose, for I am the Master of the Desert! What I demand from you is your submission to me! You will bow before me, for your life is in my hands. There is no God above me, for I am the God of the Desert!"

The cactus did not move. The poor tree was filled with sorrow. Here was a mere mortal child (for that is all he was) commanding a tree that had been around for a hundred years and that had given of itself to hundreds of thirsty, hungry travellers. Here was a mortal Prince commanding the submission of a tree that only knew one thing, and that was to "give in the name of the Origin." He or she that gives in the name of the Origin also truly understands humility.

The cactus replied to the Prince in a calm voice, "O Mighty Prince of the Desert, I salute you for you are the ruler of the land that I live in. I feel sad that you reject my humble offerings of water, fruits and shade. Indeed, they may not be as rich and clean as what your Majesty is accustomed to in the great palace. Yet, it is with my deepest Love that I make these humble offerings to you, O Great Prince. Whilst you may reject my offerings of water, fruits and shelter, you cannot reject the special prayers that I have rendered to the Origin on your behalf, for acceptance of my prayers is at the will of the Creator of All Things. With these prayers, I bid you a safe journey. May the Mercy of the Origin be upon you at each and every step of your travels."

The Prince, now filled with rage, replied, "Nobody bids me farewell at their choice. I choose who stays around me and who leaves, you insolent creature of solitude!"

"Forgive me, O Prince of the Desert, if I have offended you," cried out the cactus. "I meant no disrespect in bidding you farewell with prayers for your safety."

The Prince raised his sword and shouted, "You disobedient creature of solitude, I commanded you to bow before me in submission! You will pay with your life for your insolence!"

Just as he was about to strike the death blow, the cactus cried out, "O Beloved Prince, I meant no disrespect in refusing to bow before you in submission. I have offered to you all of myself, my leaves, my fruits and my prayers. But I cannot submit to you for I can only bow to my Creator."

The Prince replied, "If you can only bow to your Creator, then you must bow to me for I can destroy you with one single blow of my sword. I have total power at this moment over your life and death! Even the land that gives you sustenance is my kingdom. Who can be greater than me, who has power over all things in the desert?!"

The cactus calmly replied, "You are indeed great, O Prince of the Desert! But may I ask who created you, O great one?"

The Prince replied, "It was my all-powerful father and my beloved mother that created me, and it is the greatest palace on earth that shelters me."

The cactus then said, "It is indeed a blessing to have been given birth by the great Queen of the Desert. I ask thee, O Prince, who was it that gave life to you whilst you were in the sacred womb of the great Queen? Did you not start from a single Bubble of Knowledge? Did you not begin to grow your limbs, your face and all of your body after the Command was given by the Creator of All Things, for the Bubble of Knowledge to manifest itself into your Being, O Great Prince? It was not your father the great King that gave this Command. It was the Origin, the Creator of All Things that blessed you with life.

"I too, O Great Prince, grew from a Bubble of Knowledge, by the Command of the Origin. I was a spore that grew into a tree with all its branches, flowers, fruits and thorns. It is only my form that is different from you, O Great Prince. But we are both from the same Source, that which I have called the Bubble of Knowledge. My form has been granted to me so that I may be able to survive the harshness of the desert. I have been given thorns to protect me from aggressors. With the Mercy of the Origin, I have never had to use them, ever! O Mighty Prince, you have been granted the form that lets you live in the great palace. You hold your sword, which is not different to my thorns, for you have been taught to defend yourself with this sword. And yet, you stand before me today, to take my life with this very sword of defence, when I am no aggressor to you! If anything, I pray for the very best for you."

The Prince stepped back and said, "Everything that happens in this desert is by my will!"

The cactus replied, "If this is truly so, then I challenge you to create a rainshower, or maybe just create a single new cactus tree, or for that matter, heal yourself from the little wound that your sword has caused your finger! It took the miracle of Creation to make me. It took a hundred years, which may be three times your age, for me to grow to this size, O Beloved Prince. You are indeed the Prince of the Desert and I salute you as your subject. But, as you will only understand the language of royalty, I say to you that the Origin is the greatest King and Master of all, to whom alone I submit."

The angry Prince took a swift step forward and severed the trunk of the cactus tree with one blow of his cold, sharp sword. The poor tree fell to the ground gracefully, despite the humiliating blow. "Now who is the most powerful, O lifeless creature of solitude? How dare you challenge me to do anything! I am beyond challenge! I am above all things in this desert," screamed the Prince.

The cactus could feel its life leaving its body. In its final words, it said to the Prince, "You have done what any mortal could do, for to destroy is easy. You feel powerful because you have taken my life. O dear, naive Prince, it is not you who has taken my life. The time has come for me to go to live in the Eternal Garden, where rivers will flow beneath me, where flowers will blossom around me, and where I will become Everything. I will even become a part of you! But have no fear, my thorns will not prick you, for all I have learned is to love and not to hurt. Look at how weak and vulnerable you are! With a single stroke, the Creator used you as a tool to sever my trunk, so that I could join with Eternity. And here you stand, thinking that you are all-powerful for having "taken" my life. How could you possibly "take" any life when you are completely unable to "give" life? It is only the "giver" of life that has the power and right to "take" life. As I lie here on the sand, I bow in submission to my Creator, who stands before me to receive me into the Divine Light. And yet, as I lie here in front of you, all I represent to you is a symbol of destruction that you have caused. After all, you were only a tool that was used by the Origin to relieve me of the pains of solitude that I have endured for one hundred years. For this I thank you, O Great Prince. Ride back to your home in safety and may the Origin protect you, for above your head stands a Greater Sword! As the days go by, I will be buried by the sand and you will see me no more. And then will come the day when the Greater Sword will fall on your head and you too will be buried in the sand. Then we can be together again, lying side by side, next to each other. I will no longer be the cactus and you will no longer be the Prince. We will just be the equal remains of a Creation that started by the Command, through a Bubble of Knowledge. I leave with greater Knowledge than when I came into this Desert. I urge you, O Prince of the Desert, do not forget who you are, and where you came from, and to whom you will return! When I see you lying next to me under the desert sand, I will ask you what you have learned. If you reply to me with silence, I know that you will come back here to be the cactus. On the other hand, if you reply to me with greater Knowledge than I see in you at this moment of my departure, then I will be your companion in the Eternal Garden. I pray that we may be together again in the Eternal Garden, for I never wish you any harm. I would never want to see you cut down in the desert by another mortal Prince who has failed to understand his place in the Creation. Farewell, my beloved Prince.

Received on April 15, 1995.

EIGHT

*F*OOD:

THE SPIRITUAL ESSENCE OF NATURE

What does "food" mean to us all? I look around me and see people consuming food and drink at all times of the day. I see a group of four teenagers devouring their hamburgers from McDonald's with great hurry. Then, there is a lady picking away at a tub of popcorn as she awaits her bus. Next to her is a toddler sucking away at his popsicle, watched by two little girls who are happily chewing away at their bars of chocolate. A truck passes by and its driver sips from a huge plastic cup!

It is normal for us to see people constantly consuming food and drink. But what is the Essence behind the food? Is it just to provide us with energy and nutrients? It may appear to be so at the outset, however, I see a greater and broader purpose that surrounds the food that we eat....

I am sitting at the dinner table, in front of me a well laid-out plate of food — a piece of grilled steak, baby carrots, spinach and steamed rice. I am hungry and my immediate instinct tells me to carve up the beef and dig into my meal!

Then I look at the lovely baby carrots and stop. They are pretty and look happy! The carrot says, *"I am happy to have finally found my way to you. I grew up in a land far away, where you have never set foot. I thrived in fertile soil and drew all I could from it. Did you know that a beautiful deer who lived many years ago was buried in the very soil that I grew up in? She left me nutrients and a part of herself, which I also bring to you today, Amyn."*

The carrot then said, *"Did you know that there was once a cloud that travelled across the world to shower its beautiful droplets on me? How wonderful it felt, when I was touched by this blessed cloud that had collected its water from the Ocean so Pure!*

"One of the raindrops that touched me said, 'O my dear little one, I was part of the Ocean where

I lived with Myself in Infinity. I was summoned to deliver Myself to you as a blessing from the Origin. Now, you and I can be one. And although you may appear to be a little carrot, you have a part of the Ocean in you!'

The carrot then said, *"Amyn, I am also bringing a part of the Ocean to you! You will never know what part of the Ocean it is — because it is Infinite."*

I thought to myself: This baby carrot, that I previously would have consumed without any thought, has brought to me the blessings of a soil from a land that I have never set foot on, a deer that lived so long ago, a raindrop from a cloud that travelled across the world, and a part of the Ocean that is Infinite! In this little carrot has come to me Infinity!

Then the spinach spoke. She said, *"I have lived in the land of brilliant Sunshine, where I gratefully received the warm Rays of Life from the Sun. It is these Rays that made me what I am. Today, Amyn, I am honoured to bring to you the Blessed Rays of Life."*

In what appeared to be a spinach stem, which I could have consumed with no thought, I was given a part of the Sun! What a wonderful blessing!

Then it was the rice's turn. *"We grew up in different fields far and wide — so far and wide, that you would never be able to trace where each grain came from. We lived in our own fields and* were fed by different clouds. Next, we were harvested by different farmers and placed in cloth bags. Then, we were shipped to a large storage building, where we were blended with rice grains from many fields across the lands. Then we were milled and those of us that broke up were separated from those of us whose grains were intact. We were then blended again with intact grains from other lands. We found ourselves in a sack, where we spent some time together as a family. But one day, a man came with a scoop and separated us into smaller little transparent pouches — you call them bags. Then came the cook who scooped some of us from the pouch and cooked us. Once, again, we were split up into six different plates! Yet, Amyn, the wonder of Creation is that in your plate are the grains from a hundred different lands that grew up specifically to be served to you, and to become one with you! For it is said in the Book of the Universe: **'Each grain in this world has the name of he or she who is to feed from it.'"**

Now the beef spoke: "*I have lived in a land that you know not. I have been fed by the grass in the fields. I have drunk the water from the clouds. I have fed on Infinity — for that which has come from the Sun, the clouds, the Ocean and the land. Each blade of grass that I ate each day, had an origin of its own that started from Infinity. Now, here I am. I have lived to deliver myself to you. I have fulfilled my purpose.*"

I looked at my plate and thought, Nature is truly wonderful. On my plate was Nature, from the lands to the clouds to the Ocean to the Sun! The beef, the carrots, the spinach and the rice had all come from Nature, which is Infinite. I too am part of Nature. Therefore, when I consume food, a Union occurs between Nature and me. Each ingredient on my plate has a physical form and an "Essence." The Essence that is within me, which emanates from the Origin, is no different from the Essence that gives Life to the plants, trees, animals, birds and all living forms. Everything originates from the Creator, who is the Essence. That is the secret of Nature!

Therefore, each time we eat food, we Bond with Nature. We receive Union with Nature. Consider that our body has millions of living cells, all of which are alive because they carry the Essence; they have Life. And yet, through a simple meal, a grain of rice from far away, a droplet from a cloud, a part of the Ocean, and even a ray of the Sun reaches every one of our millions of cells! Is this not a Miracle? It could only be so, because the Origin created our body to be the way it is! Therefore, my dear friends, we do not eat food just for energy! We eat to Live, that is true. But there are two parts to Life — that which is material (exoteric) and that which is spiritual (esoteric)! The food that we eat reaches us in both ways.

Spiritually, each time we eat, a Union or Bonding with Nature occurs. And, we are an integral part of Nature. When we look at Life in Totality, there are millions of pieces of a jigsaw puzzle that come together. We are an integral part of that puzzle. Just as Sun, Clouds, Ocean and Earth reached every cell in my body in one single meal, I too will reach Infinity since I am part of Infinity. My body, once buried, will return to Nature and find its place in the Land, Clouds, Sun, Ocean and the Universe. The Real Me, which is part of my Creator, will return to merge into the Oneness. Then, there will be no "Me" as an "Individual Me." I will have become one with Totality, and Infinity. For this, I ever pray.

My dear friends, when you sit to have a meal, remember what I have just said. Think about it, meditate over it, for I pray that you will find the greatest of meanings from the simplest of experiences. Taking the time to sit down and share meals together with family and friends is a Divine Blessing to be enjoyed within a spirit of love and unity. Although it is common for all members of a family to walk into the kitchen and grab a bite at their own different times as quickly as possible, there is a greater joy in sitting together as a family for your meal. You will together be partaking in your Union with Nature as you eat. You will experience a feeling of great Peace and Joy as you begin to realize the spiritual

aspect of what is happening. I pray that we may be granted this special experience each and every day of our lives.

THE *Meaning* OF *Fasting*

When one is starving, it is true that one could die due to lack of nutrition. However, an added pain that occurs in the process of starvation is the loss of the Bonding with Nature. It is like a child being separated from its parent. I am sure that you have all seen the fright and terror in the eyes of a child that has lost its parent. Similarly, starvation leads to spiritual turmoil as well as physical weakness. If this is true, then why do people fast? I have often wondered why so many religions in so many parts of the world call for the practice of fasting. I have come to realize that the process of fasting creates not only a strong sense of hunger for physical nourishment, but an even greater sense of longing for the Bonding with Nature. Hence, people tend to have a heightened spiritual awareness during the period of fasting which occurs through the strong desire for this Bonding. Prayer during this period of heightened awareness leads to spiritual advancement and satisfaction.

I pray that you will treat your food with respect. Thank your Creator as you eat, for you are sharing the privilege of dining with the Divine, through the blessing of Sustenance to you. Do not ever waste your food or abuse it, for you are insulting Creation when you do so. Imagine a grain of rice that has come to you from thousands of miles away, being scraped off into the garbage bin from your plate. Just as it had finally reached its destination, you discarded it! Is this how you would treat a friend, parent, child, brother or sister that has travelled far and wide to find you? Through food, Nature comes to you in some of its most precious forms — honour, cherish and love all forms. Thank your Creator for this wonderful blessing. When you dine at home or at a restaurant, and the meal is not prepared to your liking (assuming that it is not unhealthy), eat it anyway, with honour and respect. For if you reject it, you will be turning away the Innocent and Unselfish Love that has come to seek Union with you. By doing so, you will be depriving yourself and Nature of the Bonding that had been so dearly sought! And if you should see anyone else waste or abuse their food, teach them with love what you have just learned. That too, will be a blessing.

In many religious books, such as the Quran and the Bible, it is said that the Origin has placed many Signs as reminders for us. I suggest to you that the very next meal you have is one of these Miraculous Signs. And, for all you know, it may be your last one....

Received on May 15, 1994.

NINE

THE *Blessed Tree*

There was once a cloud that travelled across the seas to a land that had been barren for many years. Upon the command of the Origin, the cloud showered its crystal-clear, cool raindrops onto the barren land. As each raindrop kissed the soil, with tenderness and purity, there was a sigh of relief from the earth, for its thirst had been quenched. Each pearl-shaped raindrop was a tender "kiss of life." This was the blessed water of life.

In the soil lay a seed that had been dormant for a long, long time. Its dry outer shell led the less wise to assume it was dead. But this dry shell contained Life, bursting to Live. Even in things that appear to be dead hides Life that is magnificent and strong. This is the beauty of Creation.

Then came a crystal-clear, cool, pure raindrop of Life that kissed this seed — a calling from the Origin that Life had come. The seed praised the Origin as it began to germinate. What was dormant and dry now began taking a form that had been blessed upon it by the Origin. And the seed became a tender seedling, with its bud gently rising through the soil. What a Mercy! The Origin had showered a million more raindrops, like Angels, to soften the soil so that this beloved and tender seedling would not be hurt as it travelled towards the surface!

The seed in humans is the child, and each fetus is protected by the blessed water in its mother's womb. What an honour it is for a mother to carry her offspring in blessed water, in which Angels hold out their tender hands to protect the little child, whose destiny has been ordained by the Origin. When one seeks Miracles as a sign to believe in the Origin, why look far! Isn't this one of the greatest Miracles?

Then the seedling breaks out from the soil and feels the first rays of brilliant, warm sunshine. What a wonder of Creation! For so long, said the seed, "I have been in darkness — dry and dormant. With the 'kiss' of the raindrop and the 'cushion' of the Angels, I am now in a Light that I never knew could exist!" Such are the wonders of Creation....

The seedling now grows into a Tree. Imagine, for so long, there had been no rain on this barren land. Now Life had been bestowed upon this beloved seed, and clouds were Commanded to travel thousands of miles to offer sustenance to this beautiful Creation, day after day, season after season. When the Origin gives Life, sustenance is graciously bestowed with it. Is this not a Miracle?

The Tree then grows to its fullest, nurtured and cared for by the Origin. Its branches now offer shade from the Sun; its fruit now offers food for all Creation. Now, travellers stop under the Tree to enjoy its shade and savour its fruit. Next, merchants collect its fruit and travel far and wide to deliver sustenance to those in lands far away who will never even know the name of the Blessed Tree that yielded this blessed fruit. This is how the Origin gives — silently and discreetly. And those that eat the fruit say, "What a wonderful taste; what a special blessing." For the starving child that eats the blessed fruit, there is an awakening of gratitude in its Soul for this wonderful blessing. Imagine, the Origin is praised and thanked by the hundreds and thousands that partake in the fruit from this Blessed Tree (whose name and location are never to be known).

This, my dear friends, is the Art of Giving. Be not known and seek no recognition. Let all recognition from the recipients of what you deliver be to the Giver of All Things, the Bestower. For, after all, the Origin gave the Kiss of Life, and Commanded the clouds to deliver sustenance to the Blessed Tree, so that it could be nourished. In turn, the Tree with all its love and sincerity delivered its fruit for the benefit and joy of all Creation. The more fruit that the Blessed Tree bore, the greater it flourished.

Received on April 25, 1994.

Therefore, my dear friends, let us be like the Blessed Tree. Let us deliver the bounties of the Origin, quietly and discreetly, to those in need. After all, the Kiss of Life has touched us. Let us never forget that! Let us also remember that the Kiss of Life was delivered through Water. Let us respect, conserve and protect this Precious Water of Life.

TEN

THE *F*RUIT FROM THE *B*LESSED *T*REE

"Little things in life sometimes carry a large meaning. We just tend to be blind to them because of our little self-centred worlds!"

When I was in Vietnam, some two or three days after writing about "The Blessed Tree," I received a physical demonstration of how the fruit from the Blessed Tree reaches people far and wide. The event that took place was rather simple, but the meaning it carried was very deep, for me at least!

My friends John, Corky, Phu and I were at the French Bistro Restaurant in Hanoi for dinner. The restaurant was crowded. Therefore, an additional table had been placed next to ours, at which sat an elderly English lady and a French man.

After dinner, Phu asked his driver to bring a bag of fruit from the car. This was a particular kind of fruit that only grew in Southern Vietnam. Phu had bought this fruit in Ho Chi Minh City two weeks prior and brought it to Hanoi, keeping it refrigerated until this evening. This fruit was unique and I did not know what it was called. It was red on the outside like a large plum. Inside, a bunch of white, fleshy, juicy seeds formed the centre core of the fruit.

The chef prepared the fruit for us and served it for dessert. It was truly delicious. In fact, with each bite, I thought to myself, I have never tasted anything so special! The experience was actually spiritual! The English lady at the next table kept looking at the fruit on our table. So, we offered some to them to taste. After she ate it, she said that as a child she used to eat this fruit but could never clearly remember its appearance or name. The taste immediately reminded her that this was the fruit she had been longing for, and kept asking about, throughout her travels across Vietnam. The expression on her face was so special! Just then, I realized that we were eating the fruit from the Blessed Tree. No one knew where the tree was, but its fruit had been carried to the market in Ho Chi Minh City, and then purchased by Phu, who had brought it up to Hanoi. The fruit had waited for us to arrive and we had been blessed with it on that evening. And the English lady — heaven only knows how far she had travelled. Yet she, too, was a chosen recipient!

Received on April 30, 1994.

As I remembered the chapter written on "The Blessed Tree," I thanked the Origin for sending the fruit from the Blessed Tree to us in a faraway place like Hanoi. For most people, this incident could be described as "just coincidence." However, I saw a very deep meaning and a clear illustration in physical terms of the inspired Chapter I had written.

I pray that we may all recognize the larger meaning in all the little things in life.

ELEVEN

THE *Golden Ring*

"Write about the Golden Ring, Amyn," I hear the Divine Voice say to me.

The Golden Ring is a symbol in the material world of a bond, or a promise. This is an everlasting promise that has its roots before birth and is like an endless tree that survives after death, into the world of the Eternal. Marriage is not a coincidence. Marriage is the Union of two aspects of the same Soul as they are rejoined while in this world.

The colour gold symbolizes the Sun and all its powers. The Ring symbolizes Unity, for a Ring can never truly be split apart. The continuity of the Ring symbolizes the strength of the bond between two people. The single Soul that divides into its two aspects, male and female, very much resembles the shape and aura of a Golden Ring. Through birth, this Ring forms its two equal and distinct halves. I emphasize the word "equal" for, indeed, man and woman are spiritually *equal*. Through marriage the Golden Ring takes its form again if, and only if, the two halves truly come together through this Union. This Union can only occur in the presence of the Light of the Origin.

When a relationship is leading toward marriage, it is essential that both the man and the woman search deeply within themselves in order to seek the approval of their Inner Selves. If this is done with utmost honesty, they *will* know if the marriage is going to be one of true Union. *The Inner Self never lies.* Unfortunately, its voice is much softer than the voice of the mind, and more often than not, it goes unheard.

If one's Inner Self is given a chance to speak through silencing one's mind for a brief few moments, the true answer will be received without a shadow of a doubt. If either of the two beings in a marriage feels apprehensive in any way whatsoever about the bond or the relationship, stop and think twice for there is most likely *not* going to be a Golden Ring. Never allow the sense of obligation to silence your Inner Voice. Remember that you have travelled a long way to find the other half of your Soul. You have journeyed through time and timelessness over lives and lifetimes. You cannot afford to be wrong! Any sense of discomfort must be taken very seriously for more often than not it is your quiet, gentle Inner Self, pleading with you.

Marriage must only be entered into when both beings feel the Love, and when the yearning for Union, with *Total Acceptance* towards one another, exists. If it is so, you will feel it, both of you. If not, you will sense apprehension and discomfort. Do not let the mind rule in such matters, for these are matters of the heart and Soul.

Allowing the mind to make decisions for the heart is like using a ten-foot metal pole instead of a paint brush to produce a painting! When an artist paints a picture, he or she uses a paintbrush and colours, for these are the correct tools for giving birth to the picture. Just so, decisions of Love must be made by the heart and Soul. They are the correct (inner) tools. If the artist were to use a long metal pole with nothing on its end to paint the picture, the end result can be imagined! Words like "ugly" or "chaos" or "confusion" are a few examples of what the end product would be! Often, when this occurs, the artist takes such a picture and discards it for it makes no sense! This is what divorce is! Then, there are artists that will try to paint the picture again with the same ten-foot pole! So they fail again, and divorce occurs over and over again! I urge you, my dear friends, to seek within yourselves the truth about the Golden Ring before you think of marriage. If it is right for you, you will know it. If not, do not ignore the truth within you that will try to caution you.

The next time you look at the Golden Ring, remember that it is a lot more than an object that you pick up from the jeweller. It represents the truth about you. It represents the Union that you have been searching for. It represents true marriage. Slip it onto the finger of your Loved One with the prayer, *"May this Golden Ring bring both of us together in the Bond that existed before our birth and that will live well beyond this Life. May we be One for Eternity."*

Remember, the term "Till Death do us Part" is a false term that must never be used. Death cannot break this Ring. It does not have the power to! Therefore, the words "Till Death do us Part" must be replaced with the words "For Eternity," because that is what the Golden Ring is. It is forever!

In a world of material plenty, our minds are so engrossed in things temporal we forget the other side of ourselves, which is our Spirit. Therefore, we make the wrong choices and more often than not, we fail. This is why the institution and sanctity of true marriage has weakened and divorce has become rampant in our lives of material plenty. There are always Golden Rings out there but it takes the heart, and Spirit, to find them. Our minds play too much of a dominant role. Our hearts and Spirits have been silenced by the terribly noisy mind. However, there is always hope!

Also, closeness to the Origin will yield a deep awareness within us of our Inner Selves. Therefore, if we were to approach our lives with this awareness, we will seldom make mistakes because we will always be "listening" to the truth within us. We must seek to be close to the Origin for that is the key to success in all aspects of Life, the material and the spiritual.

Why is it that marriages break up and result in divorces, if indeed, the bond is a deep, spiritual one? How can two aspects of the same Soul — that before birth were indeed One Soul — come together in marriage and yet part ways and divorce? The truth is, they never do separate! Once a man and a woman are united by marriage in the presence of the Light of the Origin, then they never do separate spiritually.

It is essential for people to recognize and respect the sanctity of marriage. Sex and promiscuity in this world have led people to take marriage very lightly. Such marriages fail to experience the blessing of the Golden Ring. There are indeed people who come to a city like Reno, USA, to have a great time at the casinos and to have a period of intoxication in the material plane. In the midst of this intoxication, they drive over to the "drive-in" marriage chapel and get married! This is not a true marriage because, although sermons may be read, the deep feelings of Union with the Soul may be absent. Therefore, such marriages are indeed not the marriages that fall within the Golden Ring. They are only a paper license to indulge in physical pleasures. Such marriages often do not survive. Divorce is a very easy alternative which is resorted to just as quickly as the marriage was entered into. Sometimes, children are born through such marriages. However, the spiritual Union is never complete.

What is the difference between Sex and Love? A good example would be to look at two flowers that are growing on two different trees, waiting to be pollinated. The bees may perform the act of pollination, but the fruit does not manifest. Such flowers may then shrivel and die. They are blown away by the wind, and in fact, they will have left behind no permanent mark of themselves. Then, on the other hand, there are flowers that yield fruit through the process of pollination which later become trees. These trees bear fruit again and the cycle continues. Their essence remains for Eternity.

The pollination by the bee is often driven by scent, colour and other aspects of attraction. However, the birth of the fruit is governed by entirely different principles. This is the difference between sex and Love. Sex is the bee that can be seen, heard and felt. Love is the manifestation of two aspects of One Soul that yields a permanent Bond! Love is therefore unseen, but has power that transcends a million bees!

There is also the experience of infatuation, which may have the resemblance of Love but has no depth. Infatuation is driven by physical desires and attraction. Relationships built on infatuation come and go, but leave no permanent marks. Often, infatuations lead to relationships that are so temporary! These relationships take both people in a direction that may lead them further away from the possibility of the Union with the One that they truly seek.

The Law of Karma, which says that *"Every deed or action will be met by a corresponding reaction from within the Universe,"* plays a very important role in this process. To a large extent, Karma does govern when and if the true Union will occur. Therefore, those that are deeply hurtful to others in relationships through wilful malice or neglect, will find it very difficult to attain fulfilment and Union through marriage. When things fail miserably in a relationship, take a close look at your past. One hundred percent of the time, the answer lies there. This is truly a matter of personal and internal awareness.

There are also Souls that come into this physical form that never unite, even if they are aspects of the same Soul. This type of Union is also governed by Divine Blessings and by Karma. The Union is never automatic or guaranteed. Many Souls take numerous physical forms before they achieve Union through true marriage. That is why, often, true Love is experienced by two beings and yet marriage does not occur. This true Love leaves a lifelong mark on each of the two beings, despite the fact that they may go their separate ways. There will come a time when they may be blessed with Union in one of their cycles of Life. Those that have experienced such a true Love which did not manifest into Union by marriage will clearly know what I am saying here. They have a deep yearning that has left a void or empty corner in their hearts that is crying out for fulfilment. I pray that some day they will be blessed with their Golden Ring.

For those beautiful beings who are entering into marriage, I pray that you may find happiness and fulfilment in your Union. May your Golden Ring be complete for you. May you become One Soul. May you celebrate this special day with the prayer:

> *"In the presence of our Creator, may this Golden Ring bring both of us together in the bond that existed before our birth and that will live well beyond this Life. May we be One for Eternity."*

TWELVE

THE $\mathscr{B}$UBBLE:

FIVE WAYS TO BREAK FREE

I am on a flight from New York to Johannesburg. I am served a glass of water on the plane. In it, I see ice that floats, a slice of lemon with one seed partially cut, which also floats, and bubbles of gas that cling to the side of the lemon slice. Each bubble starts small at the base of the lemon slice. It grows bigger as it rises along the side of the lemon skin, and bursts as it reaches the surface of the water. Some bubbles grow large too quickly and burst immediately. Others stay small and remain close to the surface of the water for the longest time. The aircraft shakes gently in light turbulence. This causes the lemon and the water to shake in the same manner, and at the same frequency. As the lemon shakes, bubbles that cling to its underside get released and climb quickly to the surface to burst.

I lift the glass and look below the lemon slice. There are bubbles of all sizes, which look larger than they really are because of the magnification that occurs in the water. But the gentle vibrations cause these bubbles to leave the underside of the lemon slice, where they have been stuck in their sanctuary. No sooner are they shaken off the lemon slice, they quickly rise and burst! At the surface, the small bubbles tend to survive for a long, long time. The big ones burst almost immediately upon reaching the surface. Occasionally a big bubble survives for a long time at the surface.

Alas, once the bubbles burst, they can't be seen any more. They were "real" while they existed in the water. But they are not water — they are Air! And, as they reach the surface where Air meets water, they burst, never to be seen again! They have disappeared into Air! Have they ceased to exist? Of course not, it is just that they have been transformed into a form that I cannot see anymore. They have blended into Air — into Infinity. Only because they were in the water was I able to see them. My dear friends, I am sure that you have all seen what I just saw. But what does it mean?

What I have just described is a graphic portrayal of the journey of the Soul. The bubble is like the Soul. It is made up of Air, which is everywhere. The Soul is the Light of the Origin, and the Origin is everywhere. Before the Air in the bubble entered the water, it was just a part of Air, in Totality. But, in water, it took a form. It became the shape of a bubble. Nothing changes the fact that the Air in the bubble is still only Air, as it has always been. But now, in water, it has taken a form that my human eyes can see! Therefore, it is the water that has made the Air become visible in the form of a bubble.

So, in the spiritual context, what is the water? The water is our physical form, our body. Take away the body and you cannot see Me — for I am the Soul. Give me my body and you will see a form of Me. But you are still not seeing the real Me, just as you are not seeing the Air that is contained within the bubble. There is a very close parallel that one can draw between Air and the Light of the Origin. Just as we cannot see Air with the human eye, we cannot readily see this Light. But we can *feel* Air, if we leave our skin exposed to it. If we wore a heavy sweater or coat, we could not be able to *feel* the Air.

Such is, my dear friends, the Light of the Origin. You *can* feel the Light, even when you cannot see it. But, if your actions and your deeds are not pure, they build layers and layers upon you, just as if you were wearing a million heavy sweaters! How could you possibly feel the Air then? I know without a shadow of a doubt that each one of us can feel the Light at all times — only, and only if, our deeds are pure. Just as your skin must be exposed in order to feel the Air, your heart must be open so that you can experience the Light and Divine presence of your Origin.

If I left the glass with the water and the bubbles in it on its own for long enough, the water would all evaporate and the glass would become empty. All that would remain would be Air — the Air continues to exist. Hence, the water which enables us to "see" the bubble only has a finite life. The bubble can move around everywhere in the water, and we can see it. But, once the water is gone, we can see it (the bubble) no more. Am I sad because I cannot see the bubble anymore? Of course not, because I know that the Air continues to exist. Then, why do we grieve upon the death of a beloved one? Is he or she not like the bubble? The body which gave him or her the form is gone but the Soul is Eternal; it is always there. Then why do we grieve? Here was a pocket of Air that was part of the Infinite Reservoir of Air. It then got encaged in a bubble in the water. Yes, it moved around in the water, but it was ever so limited in what it could do. Yet, when it left the water, it became once again part of the Infinite Reservoir of Air. Its presence as a little pocket or bubble in water was very temporary, just long enough to do what it had to do in the water. And then, it was gone. Will we ever be able to point out exactly where that pocket of Air went after it left the water that made it visible? No, of course not! It has become one with Totality. And yet, there will continue to be more bubbles formed, as long as the water is there. This is a very simple illustration of Life.

And, in the Name of the Origin, look at the bubbles! How many of them there are! In the water, they all start small. As they rise, they grow rapidly. The faster they grow, the quicker they rise. The bigger they grow, the greater the amount of Air they carry.

Those of us who are fortunate in this life to experience the Light of the Origin grow very quickly from within, just like the bubbles that grow rapidly in the water. The greater we grow from within, the quicker we want to free ourselves from our physical limitations. By the will of the Origin, we can rise and burst like the big bubble, to become one with our Creator again! When our Soul receives Enlightenment, our body ceases to contain and encage it anymore. We have now grown, and so fast that very soon we will merge into the Light of the Origin, like the big bubble merges into the Air.

The amount of time a bubble spends in the water is relative to its size. Some bubbles that stay small remain in water for a long, long time, even when they are right at the surface of the water; they cannot break free. But in the end by the Mercy of the Origin they will break free sometime.

On a rare occasion I saw a large bubble hang around at the surface of the water for a while before it burst. This large bubble was small when it started at the bottom of the glass of water. It grew rapidly and rose just as fast. But then, when it reached the end, just before merging with Air, it got held up in the water. There are many in this world who have risen like this. But, somewhere along their rise, they picked up a film of "dirt." The "dirt," as I call it, made the bubble stick to the side of the glass, preventing it from breaking free. Therefore, my dear friends, do not become vain or proud in success. Rising rapidly does not guarantee breaking out like all large bubbles do. And, remember, a lot of dirt can collect on a larger bubble. Hence, the larger we grow, the more humble we must become. The larger we grow, the greater the target we become for dirt, or evil. We must pray that our heart and Soul be cleansed each and every day of our lives, for the Origin is the only One that can cleanse us. We must remember the Origin in each breath that we take, for it is this Light that our Souls seek.

Look at the big bubble that has stuck to the side of the glass. How can it break free? There are *five* ways:

The *first* way is for all the water to evaporate, which may take a very long time.

The *second* way is for the bubble to receive more Air, and hence, grow larger. Therefore, if we are stuck, we should not despair, but try harder, and seek the mercy of the Origin, who will surely emancipate us, just like the bubble that gets the extra Air it needs to break free. But, if we do not recognize this, we will remain stuck at the surface, on the side of the glass. More dirt will collect on us and make us adhere more strongly to the glass. I pray that this may not be the path of our choice. I pray that the Mercy be upon us, and that the Light may cleanse us, and fill us with all that we need to break free.

The *third* way is to remove the dirt on the bubble in order to help it break free. That is why we pray to be cleansed.

The *fourth* way to break free is by the help of a gentle wind (of Air) which may blow over us while we remain stuck at the boundary between the water and the Air. This gentle wind is the help and prayers that we may receive from the beloved Souls that are around us and with us on our journey. That is why we must pray in all sincerity for the benefit of others that may be stuck at the surface, so near and yet so far! Each day, we must say a prayer for all the Souls of our loved ones and for those we do not even know, that they may be free and that they may reach their ultimate destination. Each of us can be the gentle wind that helps to set free the stuck one. And, if we should do so, we will be blessed with untold bounties, but not always of this Earth as we know it!

The *fifth* — not necessarily the last — way, is for another bubble to come beside us, and join us, so that together, we may be large enough to break away into Infinity, where there is Peace and Light. This is why human relationships are so important. Love draws us closer to one another; it creates a bond that is physical and spiritual. And when this bond occurs, two souls rise together. When we think of Love, think of the two bubbles that merged together into a larger bubble that rose rapidly. But, my dear friends, our Love must be pure. We must be honest and faithful in our relationships. A bubble that carries a film of dirt can never merge with another. Hence, purity is essential for true growth.

Received on August 19, 1994.

Let us pray that we may all be blessed with a clear understanding of the five ways by which we may obtain Freedom, Peace and Light.

begins when the sacred Union occurs in the presence
of the Origin. The physical form comes in due course
at the Command of the Origin. Therefore, my dear
friends, the act of lovemaking is far, far deeper than
we can ever imagine.

Today, I ask this special question of every woman:
*Did your life not undergo a permanent **change** after the
first time you made love to a man, through a union of
Love?* At the time that the union occurred, your womb
was blessed with a Light, a Soul that would take a
physical form in due course at the Will of the Origin.
This Light in your womb became *a part of your Soul*.
You changed from that very moment. Whether
pregnancy followed right away, or years later, is not
important. Pregnancy is just the physical aspect of the
Soul taking form. I urge you to ponder over what I am
saying. And by referencing women, I am not
excluding the role of the man. However, the woman
has the very special spiritual privilege of being a
mother. She is special, for the *Soul of her child is indeed
a part of her very own Soul*. This is why, no matter
what type of a relationship one may have had with
one's mother, one can never deny that she is, or was,
so special that no other being could resemble her or
take her place in a spiritual context. This, my dear
friends, is a wonderful Statement of Truth.

As for the man, he is an integral part of the process
of Creation of a new Life. His Soul is the one that
Bonds with that of his lover. This is the Bond of the
Promise of Life. But, once this Bond is made in the

presence of the Light, it is the *woman* that carries the new Life, in her body and in her Soul. That is why the woman has less of a primal instinct than the man when it comes to sexual relationships. A man is excited very easily and participates in the act of lovemaking or sex far more quickly and readily than a woman. While one can argue that it is a biological fact, I am simply adding, for your benefit, the spiritual dimension.

And, to my fellow males, I say, "Let us have honour in ourselves." We are the privileged builders of the Bond of Life. Let us not give away this Bond freely to everyone, for it is only meant to be given to the Soul of our beloved one. It is meant only for two Souls to cherish and enjoy. The Origin has made the entire process of making love to be most enjoyable, both physically and spiritually. However, this enjoyment has sacred boundaries that we must always respect. On a material plane, it is our privilege to have this enjoyment whenever we wish. However, there is a very clear distinction between "whenever we wish" and "with whomever we wish." We often go wrong with the "whomever" part because sex can be enjoyed with different partners at a material level, but <u>NOT</u> at a spiritual level! If all that we are aware of is the material, then we will be unable to see the difference between one lover and another.

Another thought on the spiritual aspect of making love that I wish to share with my fellow men is that each time we make love, we give away or deliver a special part of ourselves — our Seed, which is the Sacred Seed of Life. Should we not deliver this Seed to a "Pure" place? In that, my dear men, lies our Honour. Could we possibly imagine taking the Sacred Seed from ourselves and dumping it where it does not belong? When we make love indiscriminately this is exactly what happens. I urge all my fellow men to understand this. We must think twice before indulging in sex with someone we do not know or love, for by doing so, we would be giving away a most beautiful part of ourselves to a place where it does not belong. Imagine the Sacred Seed crying out to us as we indiscreetly discard it, for the few moments of material enjoyment. Where does our Honour lie in this?

On the other hand, when we make love to our Pure, destined, beloved one, the same act of making love becomes truly Fulfilling. The Sacred Seed will have been tenderly placed in the abode where it belongs, like a dewdrop that rests on a rose. Together, they are beautiful. That is what Fulfillment really means.

Therefore, to all my fellow beings, men and women, I say, do not treat sex as a primal instinct that needs to be expressed. It is a lot more sacred than that. If we were to physically meet our Origin on a one-on-one level, at a material plane, I am sure that we would not act irresponsibly, without consciousness. We would be filled with humility and respect; for the speck of dust (which is us) would have come face to face with the entire Universe (that is the Origin). When two beings Bond in Love through the physical act of sex, this sacred union always occurs in the presence of the Divine Light.

We must not treat sex as a joke for we surely know that it is an act through which a new Soul, a new Life is ordained. It is a four-part bond that occurs between the Souls of the man, woman, child and the Light of the Origin.

Remember the two bubbles I talked about (Chapter 12). If they are both Pure, they will merge, become larger and rise towards the Divine Light. Therefore, be Pure at all times in Love. I make this statement towards Love in <u>ALL</u> relationships, not just sex. But, by mentioning the seriousness of the physical act of union between you and your lover, I am conveying to you a special Message from the Origin. Ponder these words most carefully, for they will have a special meaning to you. Share this with your children, I urge you. And, if you have a shadow of a doubt, cast your mind back to the very first time that you made love, and remember and recognize that your life has truly changed since.

Received on August 19, 1994.

$\mathscr{R}$EFLECTIONS

Think of free sex with different partners in light of this Revelation, and form your own opinion.

Think of abortion in light of this Revelation, and form your own opinion.

Think of the impact of betraying the trust of your beloved ones in light of this Revelation, and form your own opinion.

Think of the beautiful garden in which flowers blossom everywhere, from pollen, to buds, to bright open petals of a brilliant array of colours, all the way through to the dry stems and flowers that have wilted. Look at this garden and then look at the hot, barren, burning desert. There are threads that connect the two. Pray that we may never come close to, or become part of, those threads.

Remember the glass of water, the bubbles and the *five ways*. Remember the slice of lemon under which all these bubbles remained trapped until they broke free. The slice of lemon is like the material world around us. If we get too engrossed in our material world, we will be like the bubbles that are just happy to stay below the lemon slice and cling to it. It will be like a cloud over us that prevents the rays of the Sun from illuminating us.

Remember the Origin and seek the Light; seek to become One with the Origin, the Most High. Be Pure and honest with yourself and with others. Let your Love for others be purer than the morning dewdrops in the garden that I just talked to you about. Merge with one another like pure bubbles and rise to Peace, Happiness and Enlightenment.

Pray for others each day so that you may be the gentle wind that helps the bubble that is stuck to break free.

Remember, you are the Light and the Light is you, just like the bubble is the Air and the Air is the bubble. You are far greater than your physical form that is limited by time and space.

FOURTEEN

THE $\mathcal{N}$EW $\mathcal{L}$AND

It was 6:00 am and I lay awake in my bed, pondering over the days that had gone by and the days that lay ahead of me. I was in a log cabin in the woods, resting my body, mind and Soul after a gruelling period of fast-paced globetrotting.

I stepped out of the cabin into the woods and saw mist resting on the green grass, tenderly caressing the trees and the shrubs. I felt the cool dewdrops kiss my feet. I felt an immense sense of inner peace as I walked towards this cloud. As I got closer, I could see the silhouette of a tall man standing in the middle of the cloud. He must have been at least six feet tall. He had long hair and a beard. He wore a robe, whose colour I could not distinguish in the mist. He did not move, but rather, waited for me to get close to Him. And then He held His arms open, as if He were inviting me into His embrace. He was a stranger and yet I felt safe and secure as I walked towards Him into the cloud. There I was, face to face with this mysterious Man in the mist. It was almost as if the cloud originated from within Him. I could not quite see His face, but I clearly noticed the glow in His eyes. He continued to hold His arms open for me. I extended my hands to Him in greeting, and as I touched His palms, I felt a strong sense of warmth gushing through my body. It was almost electrifying! "In the name of the Origin, who are You?" I asked, and then: "Why are You here, and what do You want?"

Although I could not see the features of His face, I knew that He was smiling at me. The glow of His eyes grew brighter. The mist appeared to become thinner around His being. And then He spoke to me, but not with a regular voice that one would expect from a human being. I could hear His words echo in my mind. He could speak directly to my mind, without uttering a single word from His mouth. This was a very strange form of dialogue, something I had never truly experienced before!

He said to me, *"My dear friend, I bring you greetings and Love from the New Land."* These words rang like crystal-clear chimes in my mind.

"My warmest greetings to You, too," I replied, without actually saying these words. I was also speaking directly to *His* mind! We were communicating with one another directly through our thoughts and understanding.

He squeezed my palms gently and said, *"I have come to speak to you about the 'New Land', for I know that in the name of the Origin, you will understand what I have to say to you."*

I tried hard to look at His face, but all I could see was the glow in His eyes. I could smell a beautiful incense that emanated from Him; it reminded me very much of sandalwood. It seemed as though the cloud around Him was sandalwood smoke! I looked at His feet and all I could see were dewdrops sparkling back at me. I was not afraid. In fact, I felt that there was a bond that existed between Us.

"My dear Friend, I do not know this New Land that You talk about," I said.

"Oh yes you do, Amyn," He replied!

"How did You know my name?" I asked.

To that, He replied, *"I know you much better than you know yourself."*

For some reason I believed Him! I almost felt as if I knew Him well, too! I looked around me in the mist and could see nothing but the silhouettes of the trees. Right behind my Friend, the Stranger, I could see the sparkling water of the lake. The rays of the morning Sun seemed to playfully cross the mist and cause the lake to sparkle as if it were made up of a million little diamonds.

"Who are You, my dear Friend," I asked, "and what is this New Land that You talk about?"

He squeezed my palms gently again and said, *"You are an inspired Soul. You are a Messenger of the Origin. The Divine words emanate from deep within your Soul, and you are on your way to receiving the Knowledge of the Universe."*

I could see the glow from His eyes begin to get brighter. *"When you receive inspirations from the Origin you seldom know anything about the subject that is to come to you in these inspirations. And then, you are Commanded to write down the Revelations, word by word. My dear Amyn, these words are Divine and you are to convey them to all Creation, as the Origin Wills it to be."*

As the Stranger spoke to me, I began to feel as light as a feather. I felt as if I could fly like a bird, high up in the skies. Then He said, *"The Origin has sent many Messengers to this world from people to people, language to language, nation to nation and age to age. The Divine Message has always been delivered to all Creation, by the Messengers, so that all the Souls that have been Created, from the single Unity of the Origin, may be guided directly to the Source and Origin of Everything. And yet, throughout the ages, humanity has always worshipped the Messenger rather than learned from the Message itself."*

Everything that He said to me rang a loud chord within my Inner Self, for truly, He was speaking the words that dwelled in my Soul.

"Remember, my dear Amyn, all the Messengers were simple men and women, who were nothing but the blessed servants of their Origin. There was nothing about these Messengers, in their own right as human beings, that was worthy of any worship. And, when you speak to all the Messengers, They will also tell you so. By now, Amyn, you know that you too are a Messenger. You are carrying the Message to the People in the context of this age of science, commerce and logic. And you, too, know that you are simply an ordinary human being whose Soul has been inspired by the Divine Message. You must make sure that people never glorify you, for the only glory is due to the Origin, who is the Light of the Heavens and the Earth."

By this time I could see that the glow of light had spread from the eyes of my dear Stranger Friend down to His robe, which had now begun to carry a gentle white glow. I could not help noticing the dewdrops sparkling at His feet.

Then He said to me, *"Look at my face, Amyn. Do you see my features?"*

I quietly replied, "No, O dear One, I cannot see Your features." I could feel that He was beginning to smile at me.

"That is correct," He said. *"I am here to show you that what you see in my face must be what people see in your face. I am also a Messenger, like you are. I believe that you know who I am, but you will not say it. Amyn, the absence of features on my face tells you that for a Messenger of the Origin, there must be no recognition of His or Her physical being. You see, all the Messengers could stand in front of you and all that you would see is the form that you are looking at in Me. In your eyes, I am a silhouette of a Man wearing a robe, with a glow of light that emanates from His eyes and spreads throughout His Being. The only recognizable feature about Me is the Light that you can see in My face. My dear Amyn, that is the Light of Knowledge. And all the Messengers will portray the same Light of Knowledge in Their faces. None of Them will portray any features on Their faces and, hence, you could never tell Them apart even if you tried. Your Mission in this world is to convey the Light of Knowledge to all Creation, as a blessing to humanity from the Origin of Everything. And when people attempt to glorify you, remind them that you have no facial features. All that they must see is the glow of the Light of Knowledge. This Light must permeate their inner beings and bring to them warmth and hope. It does not matter what religious beliefs they may have.*

"Remember, most religions of today arose through Revelations of the Origin which were

conveyed through the Messengers. And, if you cannot tell one Messenger apart from the other, then you cannot tell one religion apart from the other in its purest Essence. Each religion has carried the Statement of Universal Truth ('I am You, You are Me, and together We are Everything') in one form or another. Humanity's interpretation of this Statement, and the institutionalized form of religious practice has caused noticeable differences between religions. But, the Essence of all religions is truly the same. Remember, Amyn, when you look at Me, you are looking at all of the Origin's Messengers within this singular silhouette, for the Light is One. The Message that you will deliver to this world will be the Message of Oneness, the Message of Unity, based upon the Statement of Universal Truth. All people of all faiths can draw from this Message in their own contexts; yet their combined understanding of the Message will in essence be one of Unity with their Origin. Even for atheists, this message will convey the concept of Unity with Nature or whatever else they may choose to name the Source of Creation.

"The Message that the Origin is revealing to all Creation through you as the Messenger is comparable to a pyramid. All the faiths of the world collectively form the base of this pyramid, whilst the Message forms the apex of the pyramid."

By this time I knew my stranger Friend, who stood in the mist, intimately. He knew me and I knew Him. He was there to show me an incarnation of myself. It was an incarnation of no physical recognition. It was an incarnation that simply showed the Light of Knowledge. I now also knew what the "New Land" was. It was what the New World is to become. The New Land is the land of Knowledge and Unity. The term Unity refers to Unity between People, the Earth, Nature, the Universe, and the Origin. As people of this world begin to understand and live by the Statement of Universal Truth *(I am You and You are Me. Together We are Everything)*; as they begin to seek Union with their Origin; and as they begin to recognize that all Creation emanates from within their very own selves, they will begin to derive Knowledge of the Highest Order, which, in the Name of the Origin, will govern the New Land. Of course, the essence of human character is one of "Singularity" and "Difference" combined in one form. "Singularity" lies in the esoteric fact that each being is within the Oneness of the Creator. The "Difference" lies more in the physical and exoteric form of each being. A good analogy is the human body itself. No two cells are the same, yet combined, they all form one body.

As the morning Sun began to get brighter, I knew that it was time to bid farewell to my dear Friend.

"My dear Amyn, I came here to show yourself to you today. In a unique and beautiful way, the Origin has created all beings in the same way. If

you take away all the physical features from the faces of all people, and light the glow of Knowledge in their eyes, you will see that it would be impossible to tell one person apart from the other. This is the spiritual dimension of each being.

"One needs to meditate on this dimension in order to begin to recognize it. And, by the Will of the Origin, when one succeeds in achieving this recognition, it will become apparent that the Origin, Nature, and every Being form Unity. By this recognition, humanity will find harmony between themselves, their environment, and their Origin."

The mist began to thin. I had fallen in love with the sandalwood fragrance of my dear Friend from the New Land. For those that have read my description of Him carefully, you may recognize who I am talking about. But, in His very own words, He said, "We must learn from the Message and not glorify the Messenger." Hence His identity is truly not important.

In a few moments, the mist had cleared and all I could see was the sparkling water of the lake in front of which my dear Friend had stood. My feet were wet with the cool dewdrops. I could also see the sparkle of the dewdrops radiate from my feet, which served as a reminder of my dear Friend. I took a step forward and picked up a pebble and threw it in the lake. It landed with a small splash, from which grew a round ripple. Then, this ripple grew larger and larger and spread itself throughout the lake. At that point, I heard the following words of my dear Friend ring out in my mind.

"Now you understand, Amyn, the importance of the Message. You will convey to the people the Divine Words of your Origin, which will ring in their Souls like the pebble in the lake. And then the Message will spread like the ripples that grow larger and larger. And, in the name of the Origin, when these ripples reach the shores of the Lake of Knowledge, they will have led humanity to the 'New Land.'"

Received on February 19, 1995.

FIFTEEN

THE $\mathscr{L}$OST $\mathscr{A}$NGEL

The sky was a deep shade of blue. A Light that was neither bright nor dull surrounded the palace. It was a type of day that no one on this earth has ever seen. I only call it "day" because I have no other means to describe the illuminated ambiance. At the gates of the majestic palace two Angels played. Everything about them was innocent. Pure innocence. With smiling faces they played and danced to a sweet tune that only they could hear. Their movements were so gracious and their response to the music was such that one could be sure that there was an orchestra of the highest order playing for them.

They then looked at each other and while no words were uttered, I was sure that they were talking to each other. They were like innocent little babies, looking at each other. In the world of the Angels, no words are ever "said." In the world of the Angels, no distance is ever physically travelled. Purity is the only essence that richly fills their eyes.

Angels go wherever they want to, and do whatever they choose, by simple "thought." They "think" and behold, it "is." They can traverse the Universe in a flash by simple "thought." From where I stood, I could not really tell the difference between the two Angels, except that one had the form of a baby boy and the other, a baby girl. When I looked into the eyes of the baby girl, I saw a garden full of the most beautiful roses, therefore I chose to call her "Rose." The eyes of the baby boy showed me a flock of seagulls flying in the sky. Hence I called him "Seagull."

Rose and Seagull soared away into the Light for a moment. I felt sad that I might never see them again. I shut my eyes and heard the word, *"Think."* So I did! In my thought, I saw Rose and Seagull still dancing playfully in the Light. And, what a Light! There were no shadows in this Light. There was total Uniformity and I knew that this Light was Eternal. There were no days or nights. Everything was constant and the only thing one could see was Light. Now that I was in the world of thought, I could communicate with Rose and Seagull through simple "understanding." They looked at me and smiled with their sparkling eyes. I knew that they were setting off on a journey to a faraway place. But Angels can travel to any place and yet not really "move." They do not even have a form that one can compare to the physical world we know. They were like little babies whose form was thought. Hence they could be anywhere! I followed them as they travelled across barriers of time, space, matter and dimensions. They playfully continued on their journey in a manner that left me fascinated. And yet, I was travelling with them too, in thought.

Then I recognized some of the buildings and the surroundings that we were in. It was Brooklyn, New York! In the distance was a boy resting his face in the palms of his hands. He could be no more than twelve years old, I said to myself. Seagull stopped in front of the boy, who had no idea that we were actually with him. Seagull looked into the eyes of the boy, and then I witnessed one of the most beautiful sights I have ever seen. Here was a child of the earth, who looked so sad and lonely, surrounded by an aura of harshness and cruelty. And through this aura I saw the Angel, Seagull, merge himself into the boy. What a contrast I witnessed! Pure innocence, blending into harshness and sorrow. I could not see Seagull any more, but I was with him in thought.

Some distance away there was a little girl walking in the park, holding the finger of her father and smiling to herself. Around her was an aura of happiness and innocence. She could have been no more than five years old. I saw beautiful Rose merge into the little girl with the grace that only an Angel could portray.

Although I could not see Rose anymore, I was with her in thought.

Then the boy stood up and started to walk slowly. He had been crying and his face showed me a kind of sadness that I would never wish anyone to experience. This poor little child felt a pain that stemmed from the inner depths of his heart. In the side of his denim jacket, I noticed a bulge. It was a cold piece of metal — it was a gun! A gun, I said to myself? He is not even twelve, and he is carrying a gun? Does he know what it can do? Does he know that he can extinguish the life of another being with this metal object? And why is he crying?

What is he thinking about? I wondered. With Seagull having become a part of this boy, maybe I could find out! I closed my eyes and reached out in my thought to Seagull. Alas, something was wrong! In the mind of this boy were a million different thoughts, all intermeshed with one another. His thoughts were like the grey clouds that you see before a thunderstorm! In the midst of such grey clouds, one could find lightning, thunder, rain, hailstones, cold winds and blizzards. This boy did not have any real "thoughts" that were consistent and that could guide him. The poor child was in the midst of a mass confusion as the thunder clouds raged in his mind! And then there were bolts of lightning! The poor child fell to his knees and hid his face between his belly and his thighs. He covered his ears tightly with his hands. And the storm raged on in his poor little mind.

Alas, Seagull had discovered that this poor little boy had forced himself into regularly consuming a white powder that made his mind run away from everything that was around him. "They call it drugs," Seagull said. "He has to have it or he cannot bear the craving that arises from within him. The craving is sharper than the bolts of lightning that are striking every corner of his mind."

I have felt the pangs of hunger in a child that I once visited, and I can tell you that the pain that this boy feels is beyond comparison. Hunger is a lot easier to manage. He has to have this white powder or else he will tear himself apart!

I asked Seagull, "What is happening to this poor boy's Soul?" At that very point, Seagull and I began to sense a deep, deep form of sadness. We found ourselves sinking deep down into an Ocean, one whose bottom could never be reached. As we sank into this Ocean, it grew darker and darker. Seagull and I were drowning into the depths of this poor child's being. He needed help! Both Seagull and I knew the Light and the deep blue sky at the palace of the Angels. How we longed to be back in that Light. And yet, below this pitch-black Ocean that engulfed this poor child was a beautiful Soul that had also come from the palace of the Angels. How could this have ever happened? Why did his Soul sink so deep into darkness? It was like a brilliant gem whose light could no longer be seen as each layer of darkness piled itself over the other. As the Origin says, *"The recognition of the Inner Self (Light) by the Intellect will yield union with Me."*

In the case of this poor child, the intellect was damaged by drugs and his unfortunate Soul had been sunk under layers and layers of darkness. The gun in his jacket was an indicator of the evil deeds that this child had put himself through. He had surrounded himself in an environment of grief, pain and violence. And the absence of his intellect through drug abuse had only sunk him deeper down. He was not even twelve years old!

I prayed to my beloved Creator, and said, "How can we rescue this child from the torment he is in?" I felt a cool breeze begin to blow around me. It was not cold, it was cool and just right. Within this cool air began to grow a warmth that was most special. Yet, this warmth did not add heat to the breeze. I realize that in an earthly sense, these are contradictory statements! Yet all I can do is try and convey my feelings through the vocabulary of this world! Most importantly, in the midst of the cool breeze grew a special warmth. This was the warmth that the poor child so deeply needed. It was a warmth of reassurance and hope. What was so desperately needed here was "hope." I thought to myself, How could this warmth of hope ever permeate a mind that is so damaged and a Soul that is so deeply Sunk in depths of darkness?

Then, I heard the words of my beloved Origin say, *"In the midst of darkness, I can shine a Light whose brilliance could dazzle even the sharpest eyes of all."* It is only by Mercy of the Origin that hope could be delivered to this child!

Then I heard the words of the Origin say to me, *"Look, Amyn, in the depths of darkness of this child, in the midst of his confused mind, I have sent My Angel who now dwells within the cold Inner Self of this child. I will bring warmth to him. I will raise his Soul through all the layers of darkness until it breaks free into My Eternal Light. The warmth and hope will bring reason back to the mind of this child. After all, he is My Creation. His mind will focus again. His intellect will awaken again. He will be filled with Light, for that is My Decree. All My Creation is beloved to Me. They must seek Me, and seek My Mercy. By My Will, I will deliver them from darkness.*

"Say unto Humanity that they must seek their Origin. That they must seek within their Inner Selves to find Me. That they must live by the Statement of Universal Truth. Even if they are lost in darkness, hope is swift to come. After all, you thought that this child was in a hopeless situation. Now you realize that there is no such thing as hopelessness. Hopelessness is simply an appearance of the greatest depths of darkness, which you witnessed in the being of this child. And yet, you have experienced the 'warmth' in the cool breeze. You have felt the 'hope' in this breeze. For one brief moment, this little boy cried out to Me for help, whilst he was in the midst of pain and

suffering. He called out My Name. His Soul cried out to Me. And I am the All Merciful. He is my beloved Creation. I will raise him from darkness to Light, through a long staircase. Every step of this staircase will add hope in the ascension. This hope will grow into faith. And the faith will grow into the realization of the Ultimate Truth. For then there will be no more Faith. It will have become Knowledge. Eternal Knowledge."

What a beautiful lesson I have learned through this experience! In all honesty, as Seagull and I sank into the depths of darkness in the Ocean that buried the Soul of this child, I felt a sense of total hopelessness. I felt that nothing could take this poor Soul back to the Light. Nothing could clear the mind in which raged such a thunderstorm. Yet the special words of the Origin so soothingly told me that there is no such thing as hopelessness. All we must do is seek The Mercy. And we must pray that The Mercy may be bestowed on those around us who appear to be in pain, sorrow, grief and hopelessness. Even our prayers for others can help elevate them from darkness. In our interaction with those around us, we must always strive to convey hope. We must convey the warmth that lives in the cool breeze. If we pray in our own special, personal way each day for The Mercy to be bestowed upon others and ourselves, we will ascend the staircase to Light in the warmth of hope. This whole world and its people will rise from darkness and begin the ascension towards the Light. This world will become a better place. This is a Statement of Truth.

I then started to think about Rose, and the playful little girl walking in the park with her daddy. As I reached out in thought to Rose, I began to see what was happening within the mind of this little girl. At the tender age of five, this little girl had developed an immense appreciation of Nature, and the wonderful works of art of the Creator. In the park, she marvelled at the flowers, the trees, the leaves, the clouds, and everything around her. In Brooklyn, New York, such little parks are few and far between. Yet, even in this small patch of Nature, the little girl thrived in her appreciation of the Creation. In her mind, Rose could see shades of brilliant colours and forms, with reflections of spectrums of Light. While she innocently held her father's hand and looked around, she kept "absorbing" beauty in every dimension imaginable. At her tender age, she did not fully appreciate what was happening. Yet there were imprints of beauty growing in her mind with each glance that she took. Her Soul was filled with joy as she innocently continued to take in the beauties of Creation. The Knowledge in her Soul reverberated in this beauty. There was vibrancy everywhere. There was a Light within her that illuminated every corner of her being. Her intellect and her Inner Self (Soul) were in union. She was in union with the Origin. She was in the Light. She was no different than Rose. She too was an Angel.

Then I heard the Divine words of the Origin say to me, *"Look, Amyn, in this little girl there is Eternal Light. There is warmth and hope. There is no Faith because it has become Knowledge. See the vibrancy in her Inner Self. See the Union between her intellect and her Inner Self. See her Union with Me. She is at the top of the staircase to Light. And yet she is only five years old! This is where I am going to lead that little boy.*

"This is exactly where all My Creation can reach. They must learn to seek My Light. They must have a strong yearning and desire for Union with Me. They must live by the Statement of Universal Truth. There are those that are eighty years old and have not climbed the second rung of the staircase to Light. And then, there is this five-year-old who has had Union with Me. Age has nothing to do with it. My Creation can seek Me in everything that they see around them. They can seek Divine Union within their Inner Selves. And for those in darkness, I will deliver them to Light if they should seek My Mercy."

Received on February 11, 1995.

My dear friends, read every word in this chapter carefully. There are secrets to the Universe that are embedded in these Divine words. Seek them out. For those of us who see pain, suffering and hopelessness in the beloved ones around us, I urge that we pray for them. It is not necessary to go to a church or mosque or synagogue to pray for them. We can just remember the Origin wherever we are. We can say a personal prayer for them. After all, we will have helped to deliver hope to them. For those of us that are parents, let us look at our children carefully. Do we see any lost Angels?

We must help our children to seek their Origin. Let it start with Faith in the Creator. And then, by Divine Will, it will grow into Knowledge. These beautiful Angels that we have been blessed with are precious. Let us not let them go astray. Let darkness become a thing of the past. After all, we came from Light and we will return to Light, by the Will of our Origin. May we be guided through every step of our lives.

SIXTEEN

THE $\mathcal{L}$ONELY $\mathcal{B}$OY

The year is 1946. The place is Rajkot in India. The
country has been in a state of turmoil. There is strife
between the British and the Indians, the Hindus and
the Muslims, the Sikhs and the Hindus. What a time
of pain and uncertainty! Everyone has reason to fear
being who they are. In the midst of all this grew up a
young man whose name was Raju. His father was a
Hindu and his mother was a Muslim. In those days,
this was a bad combination! Raju's father featured
prominently in politics. He was a statesman and a
leader in the community. Raju learned much from his
father as he quietly observed how he dealt with a
broad range of issues amongst the people, ranging
from the very serious to the very minor. Raju had no
friends. The Hindu kids ignored him because he had a

Muslim mother. The Muslim kids did not accept him because he was not truly one of them.

Raju often asked his father, "Who am I, father, and where do I belong?"

His father, who was a wise man, said to his son, "Raju, you are different from the others in more than one way. You are much brighter than normal children of your age. You excel in your education. This makes people envious of you. Of course, they single you out because your parents are different. The problem is that they reject you out of envy and fear."

Raju replied, "But father, I am only twelve years old, and I have learned to be all alone, by myself. How dearly do I wish to play with the others. When they laugh, I wish it were me laughing. I feel the pain of being lonely. Father, what must I do?"

The years went by and Raju continued to grow up as a fine young boy. He had good looks like his father, he was bright and very successful at school. Still, he was lonely and rejected. After he graduated from University, he got an excellent job that placed him in charge of hundreds of people.

A polite and polished young man, Raju quickly rose in the corporate circles of India. He grew to become a very wealthy man. Now he was surrounded by all kinds of people who wanted to be seen with him. He was never alone, yet, he was still a very lonely man. His success and fortunes had attracted numerous so-called "friends." Even the kids that had rejected him now wanted to be with him.

One day he sat with his father after dinner in their garden. His father, who was very proud of Raju, said, "Son, you are now a successful young man. You are so popular in the community. You are their leader of tomorrow."

Raju calmly replied, "Father, it is not me that they recognize. It is my success and stature that they see. I am still the same lonely boy, who has no one he can call a true friend."

Raju's father, who had been around in all types of social circles, said to his son, "Raju, my childhood was like yours. Even as I rose to prominence, I never had any friends. I too have always been lonely. But son, you and I are born to be leaders. We breed envy in others. We overwhelm those around us. Therefore, they find every reason to reject us. Yet, we ride the crest of waves and they follow us. I have learned to find a great peace in myself. I have learned to be my own best friend. In this, I have found great joy. As I got to know myself, I also realized that I was not truly alone."

Raju said to his father, "I know what you mean. In my loneliness, I find a strange peace and comfort. This I do not find in crowds. While I lead the crowds, I still am very much with myself."

Several years later, Raju's father died. His funeral was attended by every single citizen of Rajkot. People wept for the loss of their leader. They recited praises of him at his funeral. Then Raju was asked to come forward and say a few words on behalf of the family. He started off by saying, "My father was a unique human being. He had the finest qualities, from an exceptional intellect to a compassionate heart. He always had the time to give to others. He was always there to solve the problems of others. He gave to us all nothing but love. Yet, I ask myself, what did we give to him in return? How many of us truly were his friends? How many of us truly understood him? He has gone, and yet he has brought all of us together! How can he, that was so lonely, bring together so many? This is a testimony for us all to learn from. One can stand alone as One. In that there is loneliness and peace. Yet One can also bring together All. In that too there is loneliness and peace. A leader always belongs in a league of his own. He is different from everyone. It is indeed this difference that causes others to follow him. My father was a gift to all of us. But a gift has a place of its own, no matter how beautifully it has been wrapped. Alone he came and alone he left. That is the truth about so many of us. Ask me, I would know...."

In the crowd there were Hindus, Muslims, Sikhs, Tamils and people from all sects. They all prayed for Raju's father in their own unique and different manner. As Raju heard these prayers, he said, "You all pray in different ways for the very same Soul. Today, he is one with his Origin. All your prayers reach the Origin, no matter how different we all are. Today, I rejoice in the fact that my father is no longer lonely. In the knowledge of this, I too am no longer lonely. For this, I have you all to thank. From today, I will lead you all in a manner that I have never known before. After all, a leader is also one who takes on new horizons without hesitation. Just as my father did before me, I hereby dedicate myself to you...."

Raju grew to be one of the greatest leaders of all time. Today when we look at leaders of our Nations, let it be known that there is a part of Raju in each and every one of them. Understand them well and judge them not harshly, for they have a special side to them that you know not!

Received on February 12, 1996.

SEVENTEEN

THE *D*AWN

At last, it is Dawn. Daybreak has come! A new day is about to begin. The birds are awake; hear them chirp away, telling us all their stories as quickly as they can. The dewdrops on the flowers begin to sparkle. The atmosphere is filled with Life — precious Life. There are those that sleep in their comfortable beds as this wonderful moment passes them by, for they have taken today for granted, just as they did yesterday, and will do tomorrow! Then there are those that rise with the Dawn. They look to the sky, to watch the day begin. Their hearts are filled with anticipation of the day that lies ahead.

At the harbour, a ship sets sail, gently moving towards the horizon. Its captain looks into the horizon, filled with trust that he will be guided to his destination. Then there is the farmer who sets off to the market with his produce, filled with trust that his trades for the day will bring him sustenance. Then there is the child that heads to school with a thirst for Knowledge, trusting that he may learn from new experiences of the day.

Wherever we look we see Life at Dawn. In the eyes of each being we can see trust; trust in the Origin that this new day may bring what is dearly sought, by each and every living creature.

My dear friends, Dawn marks the beginning of Life. Dawn is like birth. We come into this world with our own different missions. We trust in the Origin, that we may be guided through Life. Everything around us marks a beginning, which will ultimately lead us to the end. When we are born, we have a perception of what we are to achieve. Through Life, we follow this direction so that when we reach the end, our goals must have been met; our purpose must have been fully realized. At birth, we come with full Knowledge of the beginning, so that we may leave with the ending that we seek. But as Life progresses, as the day progresses, we forget our Mission. We lose sight of our purpose. We head towards an ending that may be very different to what we had sought at the Dawn of Life.

As the Sun rises, the day starts to take its full form. People, birds, animals and all Creation set out on their individual courses. The Sun continues its journey across the sky, and with it does all Creation move across the Earth.

During the course of the day a peak is reached by all Creation at different moments and in different ways. Then comes the Sunset, which marks the end of the journey of the day. In a similar way, the journey of Life comes to an end. Sunset is a time for Reflection, a time to think about all the events of the day. Knowledge can only be digested through *Reflection*. The events of the day have yielded experience. But Reflection converts experience to Knowledge, which can be applied in the days ahead, if indeed, there are days to come at all! The mistakes that were made, the lies that were told, the hearts that were broken, the wealth that was captured, the blows that were dealt, the victories that were enjoyed — my dear friends, Reflect and Reflect so that you may learn from this day. Look at what has happened! How much joy did you bring? How much happiness did you give? What good did you do? How many smiles did you generate around you? Reflect, oh please, Reflect!

Through the Mercy of the Origin, we have been given this day. And by this Mercy we may have the benefit of Dawn again tomorrow. Let us live by the words of the Origin, which say, *"If Dawn is the start of Life, which stands on pillars of trust, then Dusk is the end of Life that must stand on pillars of accomplishment."*

The time in between Dawn and Dusk is ours to savour. We must fulfill our purpose before Dusk, so that when we should Reflect over our lives, there must be no remorse. There must only be the joy of having fulfilled the purpose for which we were given this Life. And, behold! Look at the number of chances that the Creator has given to us! How many Dawns were we blessed with? How many Dusks did we Reflect upon? How much did we learn? What did we do with that Knowledge?

Are we prepared for the Ultimate Dusk? If not, let us look to tomorrow's Dawn as another chance. And when tomorrow's Dawn comes, let us remember that it could be our last Dawn. Let us lead our lives as if each day were to be our last day in this world. Let us set our priorities accordingly so that we may differentiate between what is important and what is not; between what is good and what is bad; between what is right and what is wrong.

Remember that the first Dawn of our lives, our birth, started with trust. We can see this trust each day of our lives if we care to look around us at Dawn! Let the Origin be our Guide. Let us remember and trust the Origin at all times.

Received on September 23, 1994.

I pray that we may be blessed with a constant awareness of our purpose in Life. May we be led by the Origin to pass successfully through the maze of Life, where crossroads of good and evil stare at us with every step that we take.

May we always be guided along the Right Path, for our entire Life is as good as one day. It starts with Dawn and ends with Dusk. Let us take every new Dawn as a special blessing, a special chance that will give us yet another opportunity to reach the Ultimate Dusk, when we can break free to become One with the Light of the Origin.

EIGHTEEN

THE *Horse Race*:

A Story of Human Nature

The race was about to begin. All the horses stood anxiously behind their gates. The favourite was a black horse called Black Stallion, on whom lay the best odds of victory. The second favourite was a brown horse called Desert Sands. Somewhere along the way stood a white horse, whose odds of victory were way down. Its name was Milk Trail. The name of Milk Trail's jockey was Henry. The race was about to start. The excitement level in the crowd was rapidly growing. Henry sat calmly on his horse with no anxiety whatsoever. Over time Henry had learned that the best attitude towards any contest in life, or any situation in life, for that matter, was to have no expectations. His philosophy was simple: "There can be no disappointment in life if you hold no expectations and do not cling to a desired outcome from any event." He was a firm believer in the principle of "Let it Be" and "Accept and learn from the outcome of every situation."

Just then, the crack of the gun was heard. All the horses came dashing out of their gates. Almost immediately Black Stallion took the lead. The crowd cheered loudly. Desert Sands took third place right away. Milk Trail pulled off a steady start in 9th place. Henry knew that all the cheering from the crowd was not for him. All the eyes of the spectators were fixed on Black Stallion and Desert Sands. There was a lot of money that had been bet on these two horses. In a prime spot in the spectator's deck sat a father and a daughter. The father, Charles, had bet 500 British Pounds on Black Stallion. His daughter Susan, who was only nine, sat and watched the race with no knowledge of any bets whatsoever. Susan's joy was simply to watch each horse perform in its own way. Her father's eyes, however, remained fixed on Black Stallion and he was oblivious to all other horses in the race. For Charles, this was just a one-horse race, and he had all his money riding on a single horse.

As the race progressed, Desert Sands increased its pace to claim second place, right behind the heels of Black Stallion. Milk Trail also began to gain, climbing up to sixth place. Charles' heart began to sink as he watched Desert Sands start to overtake Black Stallion. Little Susan on the other hand was fascinated with Milk Trail. She said to her father, "Look at that white horse, Dad! It was right at the back of the pack and it has moved up to 6th place! What a performance, Dad!"

Charles was somewhat irritable and said, "Susan, I am not interested in the back-runners. Those are the losers! My bet is on Black Stallion and that silly brown horse is about to make me lose my bet! I wish it would slow down!"

Susan, who was somewhat confused, said to her father, "But Dad, I thought we came here to see all the horses perform in a race! That white horse has performed better than any other! Your desire to have Black Stallion win by wishing for the brown horse (Desert Sands) to slow down is not part of what a race is all about, Dad!"

By this time Charles was livid because Desert Sands was in first place. He snapped at Susan and said, "Be quiet, Susan! This is bad! My horse is losing and my money is gone, just because of that brown horse!"

Little Susan, who was almost in tears, said to her father, "But Dad, I thought we had come here to have fun and watch all the contestants perform! And now, you are upset and mad! This is not fun!"

By this time, Desert Sands was way in the lead. Charles looked at his daughter and said, "This race is not fair! I've lost my money! All you can admire is a white horse who is a loser, who has made some progress! I hate losers!"

Susan quietly said, "If you knew how you wanted this race to end, then why did we come here in the first place? I don't think any of the horses or their jockeys are losers! They are all trying to do their best! Did you and Mum not always tell me that winning is not everything?"

By this time, Charles had realized that he had upset his daughter. "Yes, Susan, winning is not everything. I bet on Black Stallion and wished that he would win. I am not happy because I am about to lose my bet, that's all!"

Susan replied, "Are we here to watch a race or to make money, Dad? That white horse was last and now he has come to fourth place. I think he is a winner, not a loser!"

In the meantime, Henry carefully watched the three horses that ran ahead of him. He was calm and Milk Trail was with him all the way. He then said to Milk Trail, "We can do it, Milky — we can win this race!"

The white horse replied, "But all of them out there don't want us to win! They are only calling out for Black Stallion! They do not want us to win!"

Henry replied to his horse, "Milky, it does not matter what they want. What matters is how well you and I perform. This is our race, not theirs! Look at those strange people in the front row with their funny hats! Can you imagine where they would be if they were running in this race rather than standing back there and yelling out for Black Stallion!"

The horse replied, "That would be funny for sure! Henry, let's do it!" With that, Milk Trail dashed forward and overtook Black Stallion to move into second place.

Susan, who could barely contain herself, said to her father, "Look, Dad! My white horse is in second place. It is not a loser!"

Charles replied, "It doesn't matter anymore — I've lost my money! This race is over for me!" Milk Trail took another series of power strides and overtook Desert Sands. The crowd went silent! How could this be? This was not supposed to happen! While Milk Trail and Henry put on the best performance of their lives, there was a crowd largely dismayed and unhappy! A lot of money was about to be lost!

The race ended with Milk Trail well ahead of all the others. There was no enthusiasm in the crowd! Black Stallion ended up fifth and its poor jockey, who had been very used to winning, left the field with his head bowed down in shame. Charles grabbed Susan's hand and began to exit the stadium. Poor Susan, who was so elated, broke free from her father and ran towards Milk Trail and Henry. She patted Milk Trail fondly and said, "Well done! You are the best! I watched you from start to finish — you were the best!"

Charles followed his daughter and came over to Milk Trail. He said to Henry, in a dejected voice, "Well done!"

Henry replied, "I am sorry we caused you to lose your bet!"

Charles, who was somewhat embarrassed, said, "That's okay! Next time I'll bet on you!"

Susan quickly replied, "Oh Dad! Please don't do that to this lovely horse! That poor Black Stallion lost the race because it was treated like the only real horse in the race. Let Milk Trail run again, with pride and not pressure! Why don't we bet on other things, Dad, like maybe who can clean up the dishes the fastest at home!"

Henry got off Milk Trail's back and put his arms around his dear horse. "Well done, Milky," he said.

Milky, who looked somewhat sad, said, "Will you still love me if we don't win the next time?"

Henry replied, "Why on earth would you say such a thing, Milky?!"

The horse replied, "Black Stallion's jockey was hugging him before the race and yet, after they lost, he looked at Black Stallion with anger and hatred in his eyes. I would rather never race again than lose your love, Henry!"

Henry hugged Milky and said, "Winning and losing is not really important. We are a team and we will always do our best. I love you today, and will love you always. Do not forget that, Milky!"

The horse then said, "Why are you so different from other human beings? As we ran, there were thousands of people who cheered and loved Black Stallion. And when he lost, they called him names and walked away!"

Henry replied, "Milky, it is not Black Stallion that they loved. In the world of the humans, there are funny pieces of paper called money. It is this paper that they love. If Black Stallion won, then they would win more funny paper. But, because Black Stallion lost, they too lost all their paper. So, Milky, their love has nothing to do with Black Stallion. It is all about money."

The poor horse was bewildered. It said, "Because we won this time, will all those people put their beloved paper on us the next time? Will they cheer us even if they don't really care about us? Will they cheer us because we can win them more paper? Whom are they really cheering, us or their paper or themselves?"

Henry replied, "They are all very selfish. They really don't care. To them this is not a race! To them, we are just objects that can be used to make them rich! There is no question of love in their eyes. It is only money and greed. But, Milky, we will not let that get to us. We will run again and try our best. Our joy is to do our best, that's all we care about. Do not try to win their love because you will never be able to. If you win them paper, they will want more from you. As you give them more, they will expect even more. This does not end, my dear Milky!"

The horse looked at Henry and said, "At least you love me regardless. Please promise me that you will never bet on me, ever!"

Henry replied, "I promise you, Milky, I'll never bet on you. You will never lose my love."

Milky then replied, "Will they ever change? Will they ever learn to love us for what we are?"

Henry shrugged his shoulders and said, "Not likely, Milky!"

The horse sadly looked at the spectator area. In the distance he saw Susan waving at him. His heart leaped with joy as he said to Henry, "That little Susan loves me! You see, there is hope — they may change!"

Henry replied, "Yes, Milky, there is hope!" Then Henry turned away from Milky and said to himself quietly so that the horse could not hear him, "She is little. Wait until she places her first bet on a horse. She will become like the rest! If only you knew humans, my dear Milky!"

The horse, who was not supposed to have heard this comment, said, "I heard you, Henry! But I don't believe Susan will change. And as more people learn about the story of Milky and Henry, there will be more Susans around! Believe me, there will be many, many more Susans around. Henry, there will come a time when we will be truly loved for what we are.

Paper will not matter! That is the power of the story of Milky and Henry!"

With a smile on his face, Henry said, "Milky, I pray that you are right. I pray that this acceptance in people will grow from horse racing to business to all forms of relationships in this world. Isn't it funny, Milky, we never dreamed of winning a race, and yet, here we are, dreaming of a major change in the world."

Received On June 17, 1995.

In this simple, light-hearted story lie numerous aspects of our daily lives which shape our attitudes towards people and events. Let us look into the story and ask ourselves if we see a Henry, a Milk Trail, a Black Stallion, a Desert Sands, a Charles or a Susan in our lives. Which one(s) of these characters is us? Let us Reflect.

NINETEEN

THE *S*TORY OF THE *M*ERCHANTS

*"When you give more than you take,
you Create."*

In the ancient city of Constantinople lived a merchant whose name was Tiberius. In the narrow street each morning he opened the doors of his shop, from where he traded jewellery and spices for clothes and various food items. Each day he would be visited by customers from the city and from places far, far away. Tiberius was known, even in the most distant lands, to be one of the fairest merchants of Constantinople. His scales and measures were always tilted slightly in the favour of his customers.

From China sailed a spice and oils trader by the name of Lee. He carried with him spices from all over the

Orient. He carried some of the rarest oils and incense. Lee was a very intelligent and shrewd merchant. As a child, he had started life with practically nothing. He traded in small things each day and slowly grew to become a trader who travelled to faraway lands in his own ship. For Lee, every trade was a challenge that he had to win. Every trade was a means whereby he could end up with more than he started. For Lee, every trade was a process of "accumulation." He always took more than he gave. He seldom cared about the people that he traded with, so long as he came out the winner each day. For Lee, there was no such thing as defeat. For Lee, there was no such thing as loss. All he cared about was winning. He was not popular among the other merchants because of his "killer instinct." However, he was respected by many for his success and wealth.

On the early morning of February 8, in the year of 1012 AD, he set sail for Arabia and Constantinople. His ship was filled with valuable merchandise. Lee's philosophy was never to leave anything behind. He would fill his ship with *all* his merchandise. He would return home with more. Yet, while he was out at sea, everything he owned was truly at risk. This did not bother Lee at all because he had never accepted the concept of "loss."

One night during his journey he sat on the deck of his ship and looked out at the stars. He started to count them. He kept counting them for hours, but they never ended. What kind of Merchant is it that lives in the Skies, and owns countless stars? he thought to himself. He looked at the scroll of paper that showed his inventory on board. It took him fifteen minutes to review one hundred percent of his inventory on board. Yet, it took him hours to try and count the countless stars. He cried out to the dark sky, "O Merchant of the Skies — I would like to meet You someday; I would like to trade with You. You can show me how to own countless things!"

The cool wind of the night slowly made Lee fall asleep. He woke up to the rays of the bright morning sunshine. He remembered speaking to the Merchant of the Skies. He wanted to meet this Merchant whose property had no limits!

As he ate his breakfast he looked into the Ocean and saw a large school of fish. He started to count the fish and quickly realized that they were countless! How many fish are there in the sea? he asked himself. Here was the Merchant of the Ocean, who also owned countless fish. He called out to the Ocean and said, "O Merchant of the Ocean, who are You? How do You come to own this unlimited number of fish? I would like to trade with You, so that I could learn to own unlimited property!"

Later in the day, he sat on the deck of his ship and looked at the glittering waves as they reflected the rays of the Sun. He started to count the glitters. They were unlimited. Once again he looked into the sky and cried out, "O Merchant of Light, how could You own these countless numbers of rays? I want to trade with You so I can learn to own countless possessions!"

His boat landed on the Arabian coast after a few days, where he set about trading his spices and oils for dried foods and jewellery. He met a young boy named Salim, who offered him a pouch full of diamonds in exchange for his spices and oils. Struck with awe, he asked Salim, "Where did you get these stones from?"

Salim replied, "A merchant from Africa brought them to me. He said that he had dug a hole in the ground and found countless stones like these. Of course, he could only carry away as many stones as his ship could contain!"

Lee said to Salim, "Did you say countless stones?"

"Yes," replied Salim. "But the poor man could only carry away as many stones as his ship would allow him to carry!"

Lee looked at Salim and said, "He was limited by the size of his ship! He found countless stones, but he was limited by himself! What a shame!"

That night as Lee sat on the deck of his ship he looked at these beautiful diamonds as they twinkled in the starlight. All of a sudden, he had visions of the big hole in the ground where these stones had come from. The stones were beautiful. They were pink, white and blue. He started to count them, but they were countless. He cried out, "O Merchant of the Earth, how could You possess such unlimited stones? I would love to trade with You so that I may learn how to acquire limitless possessions!"

Then, he looked around him and once again noticed the stars. "Could the stars be stones like these diamonds, that belong to the Merchant of the Skies?" he asked.

Surely, the Merchant of the Skies has traded with the Merchant of the Earth! As he looked at the twinkling stars, he noticed that they gave off millions of soft rays of light. He thought to himself, the Merchant of the Skies must also have traded with the Merchant of the Light, for those stars are giving off countless rays of Light!

He looked around his ship at his precious belongings and realized that everything he possessed was limited to the size of his boat! Maybe I should have a bigger boat, he thought to himself. The bigger my boat gets, the more I can possess. But how big should my boat be to make my possessions limitless? He could not even imagine such a boat.

Once again in the morning he was visited by the countless fish. Once again he was faced with the Merchant of the Sea. He cried out, O Merchant of the Ocean, how did You come to possess these countless fish? What is your secret? You can have all that is on my boat in exchange for Your answer!

Then he heard a loud Voice in the Ocean say, *"Lee, if I answer this question, you will not be able to see this answer with your eyes. All it will be is 'Knowledge' in your mind. You cannot touch it and feel it like you do your merchandise. Are you willing to trade all your possessions that you can touch and feel, for Knowledge that you cannot see?"*

Lee thought for a moment and said, "From what I have seen of the Merchants of the Ocean, the Earth, and the Skies and the Light, I cannot say that my precious few possessions in my little boat can have any value compared to Them. No boat that I build could ever be big enough to trade with Them. Therefore I will take "Knowledge" in exchange for my possessions, for whatever it is, it has far greater value than everything I have worked for all my life!"

The Voice of the Ocean replied, *"Lee, you are a very smart trader for you can see value in something that no other merchant could recognize. I will now trade you the answer so long as you are absolutely sure that you are willing to pay for it with all your possessions!"*

Lee replied, "I am ready to do the trade. Tell me the answer."

The Voice replied, *"As the Merchant of the Ocean, I possess countless fish because I CREATED them."*

As soon as Lee received the answer, his boat was empty. Yet he felt enriched. He felt wealthier than ever! He asked himself, what have I ever CREATED? All I have done is to take and to trade one for another. I was limited by the size of my boat and by the quantity of what I had to trade. But, I CREATED nothing. More so than the size of my boat, I was limited by the size of my mind! Now I have traded my little possessions for Knowledge. With this Knowledge I will CREATE.

A few weeks later, Lee found himself in Constantinople. He visited the shop of his friend Tiberius. He sat in the shop and watched Tiberius do his trades. He noticed that

Tiberius always gave a little more than he took. Yet how could Tiberius possibly flourish?

At the end of the day Tiberius invited Lee to dine with him at his home. Tiberius had a lovely wife, Emma, and six children. As the two friends ate, Tiberius said to Lee, "I noticed that you have come here with nothing to trade, yet you look richer than you ever did before. Therefore I presume that you must have done a good trade with someone."

Lee replied, "Yes, my dear friend, I did a trade with the greatest Merchant ever!"

Tiberius replied, "I can see that." Lee had changed and Tiberius had immediately noticed this change in his friend, who visited him regularly from China to apply his "killer instinct."

Lee asked Tiberius, "Tell me, my dear friend, did you always deliberately give me more than you took from me each time we traded?"

Tiberius replied, "Yes indeed, my friend. I always gave you more than I took from you. Is that not why you kept coming back to me?"

"Yes," replied Lee, "that is true. I came to you because I always gained from you! Is that why merchants from all over the world come to you?"

Tiberius replied, "Yes, I always give more than I take; not just in merchandise but in everything I do. Each time you give more than you take, you CREATE."

Lee was astonished with this answer. He then asked, "If you give more than you take, how can you possibly flourish? Why don't your stores become empty?"

Tiberius smiled and replied, "When you give more than you take, all that you retain for yourself gains quickly in value. Therefore, when you trade it again, you are trading a greater value. You can keep giving more than you take, for your value grows with each trade. As people receive more from you, they always come back to trade with you. You start to enjoy limitless trade. And the value created from these trades reaches into the homes of limitless people throughout this world. This is how I CREATE."

The astonished Lee said to his friend, "When you CREATE, you produce something from nothing, don't you?"

Tiberius replied, "Yes, that is true, sometimes. But also when you give more value than you take, you have also CREATED something. This creation is not limited to the size of any ship for it flows by itself to all corners of the world." Seeing his friend deep in thought, Tiberius asked, "Tell me about this great Merchant that you traded your entire merchandise with? Who was He?"

Lee quietly replied, "He was a limitless Merchant with countless possessions. You have met with Him, haven't you, Tiberius?"

His friend smiled and replied, "Yes, I have met with Him. I have seen Him in the Ocean, in the Skies, in the

Earth and in the Light!" Lee could not believe what he was hearing!

Tiberius then took Lee over to one of his storage rooms. As soon as he unlocked the door of the room, Lee recognized all the merchandise in it immediately. "This is everything that I traded with the Merchant of the Ocean," he exclaimed!

His friend replied, "Yes indeed! You traded all this for Knowledge. You became rich with this Knowledge. Now you can have your merchandise back. You can start to trade again. But remember, you must CREATE. That will make you limitless. You will own countless possessions within yourself and around you. Remember, merchandise is only a vehicle for you to CREATE. Give freely of yourself, your love and your kindness for that is what makes you limitless. Remember, the fisherman takes from the Merchant of the Ocean. What does he give in return? The miner takes from the Merchant of the Earth. What does he give in return? We all take from the Merchant of Light. What do we give in return? Our ships are all guided by the Merchant of the Skies. What do we pay in return? Who is the Giver and who is the taker? Who is indeed the CREATOR?"

The next day, Lee loaded his ship with the diamonds, fabrics, oils and spices. As he bid farewell to his friend, he said, "How could I ever thank you? You have taught me so much!"

Tiberius replied, "You recognized the value of Knowledge. You recognized the greater dimensions of yourself. You traded all your possessions for this Knowledge. After all, did you not say to the Merchants of the Skies, Ocean, Light and Earth that you wanted to trade with them so they could *teach* you to achieve limitless possessions?"

"Yes," replied Lee. "Yes indeed!"

Tiberius then said, *"Well, Lee, I was listening…."*

Received on February 12, 1996.

TWENTY

THE &AGLE

As I looked at the sky, against the backdrop of the midday Sun I saw a large, strong, majestic Eagle soar below the clouds with decisive direction and speed. Here was a bird that had been bestowed with such great strength, beauty and power. As it spread out its wings, it displayed the full image of the source of strength for its flight. Look at the wonders of Creation, I said to myself.

I then heard the Divine Voice say, *"We have created the Eagle as a symbol of strength. It will soar high in the skies for all Our Creation on land to see. It has eyes that are sharper than those of the finest creatures on Earth. It can seek out its prey with such precision. These are the tools that We have bestowed upon the Eagle. It can collect its sustenance with grace as it dives down to receive its prey. There are very few of its prey that ever have a chance of winning in the battle with the Eagle. This is a bird of Strength and Pride. But this bird is not vain. This bird feeds on its prey as and when it needs sustenance. It does not use its strength and power in the skies to come down and terrorize creatures for no reason. This is an example of the correct and appropriate application of strength in Nature. Amyn, there is a lot that one can learn from the Eagle."*

I continued to watch this majestic bird. It soared with great speed and yet it did not seem to be in any hurry at all! Then, once again, the Divine Voice said to me, *"Have you watched the behaviour of human beings when they are bestowed with power and strength? Have you looked at how easily their pride and vanity takes over? Do you see how indecisive a man or a woman is compared to the Eagle? Do you see how human beings rush along with great haste in Life, whereas the eagle moves more swiftly, with no haste? You see how the Eagle only uses its strength for getting its sustenance and protecting itself? Look at humanity! The stronger ones bully the weaker ones. At the first available opportunity, the stronger ones impose their will on the weaker ones.*

"We have granted humanity strengths in the form of physical strength, intellect and a full range of skills. These strengths are to be used for a specific purpose, to enable each being to succeed in the

fulfilment of his or her Mission. Yet, you will see more skills abused than used correctly.

"Look at the Eagle in the sky. It gives lessons for the wise ones to learn from! From its place in the sky, the whole Earth is its domain. It looks down at people and creatures as it proceeds through its journey. It sees people fighting for material possessions on land, whilst it praises its Origin for granting the entire Earth to be its domain. This can be so for humanity, too! But human beings have to first rise like the Eagle in their Spirit and then look at the Earth as their domain. Just then, they will realize that they are greater than the Eagle, for their domain is indeed the Universe."

Received on July 23, 1995.

TWENTY-ONE

EATH

"Death is the continuation of that which was interrupted by birth.

Life in this world is but a short stop in the passage of Eternity."

It was a bright sunny day as I boarded the train en route to a destination that lay far, far away. I had come to this train station from a distant place and was headed to a place even further away. Yet, I was very clear about the destination that lay ahead of me. I was also very much aware of the multitude of aspects of Knowledge that resided within Me. This Knowledge I had collected throughout my journey of many lifetimes, and yet, in the name of my Origin, there was more to come! As the train departed the station, I sat back to enjoy the magnificent scenery that surrounded me. It was the Perfect Picture, drawn and painted by the Ultimate Artist. And I was very much a part of this Picture. I could look at it from outside, and at the same time, I could be within it. What a wonderful Picture! I had no schedule to keep, no urgency to deal with; I just travelled within this magnificent Picture. But, all along, I knew that I was on a long journey that had neither truly begun, nor would truly ever end. I was "Eternal." And within the Picture of Eternity, I was whole, complete, happy and free. There was nothing that I desired because I *was* Everything. How can you ever desire something when you are Everything?

And then the train stopped. Ahead of me, I could see the most beautiful Garden that ever was. I got off the train to head into this lovely land of Paradise. But just then I turned away to look at the green rock that lay on my right side. At that point, for one very short moment, I was out of the Picture of Eternity!

I found myself born into another Picture, in which I did not truly belong. All I could do was to look at this new Picture. I was in a shell called the human body. I was not free. I was encaged! Around me were others who I called my parents and my brother. Then there were friends. As I travelled forward in this new Picture, which to me was "unreal," I experienced joy, sadness, love, pain, anger, peace and everything that the Picture had for me to experience. I was no longer "Limitless." In fact, I was totally limited within my shell. Then I had a wife and four children. At some point, I recognized that

I did not belong in this land of the "unreal." I often had glimpses of who I really was.

Yet in this "unreal" world, I set forth to do many things to bring a touch of the "Real" to all Creation. In doing so, my life unfolded into new directions as each day went by. My shell was aging. Everything in this "unreal" world was governed by an invisible element called "Time." No one could see it, but everyone lived by it. Time had set its laws for the encaged to follow. And yet, for the encaged, as each portion of Time passed by, they moved closer to freedom; freedom from the cage, freedom from Time itself.

What did I do? How did I impact this "unreal" world? What did I learn from it? What did I give to it? My life was like a scroll that unfolded each day with Knowledge, wisdom and hope. Of course there was pain and suffering. But the writing on the scroll was that of purity, and nothing but purity. Yet, the dirt from this "unreal" world left stains on my scroll as it unfolded. I desperately tried to clean off each stain before more of the scroll unfolded. It was by the Will of my Beloved Origin that each stain was removed through Divine forgiveness. I learned to guard the scroll from future stains by learning from my mistakes.

As I grew older, the hair that grew on my shell began to turn grey. And, as I looked around me, everyone that had grown up with me was also turning grey. They all knew that this strange and invisible Time would run out for them. And yet, they feared that very moment when Death would come to greet them. How could they fear the end of what is so temporary? After all, do we truly belong to this invisible Law of Time? We were never part of it. Yet, for this one short moment in Eternity, which we call a Lifetime, we were under its umbrella.

Then, one day, I lay on my bed and looked around me. My time had come to leave this world. There was my family, my wife and my children, sitting next to me. They all looked very sad. And, yet, I felt nothing but happiness. As I looked into their eyes, I prayed for their freedom from this "unreal" world. I could hear them say to me that they loved me. But then, each word grew softer and softer until I could hear no more! Their lips moved, and all I could do was watch. Suddenly, I began to feel very, very light. I began to rise from the shell and I could see very clearly and also hear what was being said with total clarity. I had never heard, seen or sensed everything so clearly for all the time that I had lived in this "unreal" world. I had left my shell. I could see my loved ones shed tears over my departure. To them, I had died. If only they could see how happy I was! I could now see through their eyes, hear through their ears and feel through their hearts. I was a part of them. I was closer to them than I had ever been, or could ever be, while I was in the shell. I knew that each one of them would enjoy the experience of breaking loose from the "unreal" world when their time came.

Now that I had left my shell, I could no longer command it to do anything for me. I was a free, white dove, with strong wings and no desires for I had become Everything. Why would there be any need for me to command the shell to take me places or do things for me, when I was in fact Everything!

I was now back in the beautiful Picture of Eternity. I turned and looked ahead of me. Oh, yes, there was the train, and in front of me was the beautiful Garden that I was heading towards, until that brief *interruption* that occurred when I turned to my right to look at that green rock! I was glad to be back in the Ultimate Picture, painted by the Ultimate Artist. There was no longer this invisible Time, nor any elements of the "unreal" world that I had just left. Of course, when I think about it, I had only left the Picture of Eternity for a very, very short moment, as I walked towards the Garden. Under the laws of Time, it only felt like a fraction of a second. And then, I was back doing what I had always done; I was back on my journey. Of course, I took with me the "experience" of that brief moment in the "unreal" world. That experience had become Knowledge, which added itself to all the Knowledge that I had accumulated so far.

After a peaceful walk through the Garden of Paradise, I boarded the train again and was on my way. I reflected on my brief moment in the world of the "unreal," as I had turned to my right to look at the green rock. All it was, was an interruption that was caused by my birth into that world. And of course, death from that world put me back on the continuation of my journey through Eternity.

In the "unreal" world, I was told that when I died, I would lose all my senses: hearing, smell, sight, touch and everything else. I smiled to myself as I thought of this statement while I travelled on the train! If anything, I had lost ninety-nine percent of my senses when I came into that shell, that cage they call the human body. And, with Death, I had got back all my senses. What a myth about the five senses! And, how naive were we to think that these senses were the most important. If only we could have remembered the senses that we had lost through encagement! We had gone from freedom and Light into confinement and darkness! We had gone from being Everything to becoming only "something." Of course, I also realized that had I tried to discover Myself even while I was in the shell, I may have been able to enter the Ultimate Painting whenever I wanted to, because I would have been able to differentiate between the Illusion (the material) and the Real (the eternal). But how could I have done that? I was too engrossed in the ways of that world. I was governed by this invisible Time.

Of course, in the shell, all I could use to "remember" was the mind that resided in the shell. That mind could never "remember" what it had never experienced! But if my mind had been able to become one with my Inner Self, then I could remember Everything, for my mind would have then *experienced Everything.* **"Connect the intellect to the Inner Self and you will Discover Yourself, Your Creator and the entire Knowledge of the Unlimited."** I had heard these words as I resided in my shell. I shared them with others, in the prayer that they would all achieve this realization.

Received on December 29, 1994.

My dear friends, for those of us that live in this "unreal" world, may we open our minds and hearts and take in the words that this Chapter rings out to us.

May we never fear death. May we remember that it is a special experience that leads to freedom of the Soul. After all, **"Death is a continuation of that which was interrupted by birth."** *Life in this world is a very, very short interruption. Our true journey is long and exalted.*

TWENTY-TWO

THE $\mathscr{L}$OSS OF A $\mathscr{C}$HILD

It was early afternoon as I looked out the window of my cottage towards the vast blue Ocean. The cottage sat on top of a Cliff in Nova Scotia, Canada, surrounded by hills and mountains and the blue sea. The rocks along the Cliff were sharp and jagged. The Cliff faced a small cove, and a short distance away from the shore a rocky Island sprang up from the bottom of the Ocean. There was some vegetation on it, but primarily, the entire landscape was comprised of sharp rock. I gazed at this little Island with its peak that rose perhaps one hundred feet above the water level. The waves kept crashing against this Island mercilessly, as they did against the base of the Cliff below my cottage. The overall atmosphere was tranquil except for the crashing waves. Just then I began to hear whispers which sounded like two members of a family sharing some form of a secret. I looked around the cottage and outside, but could not see a single Soul. I stopped and listened carefully. What I was listening to was a conversation between the Cliff and the Island! The only other sounds that surrounded the whispers were those of the wind and the waves. I sat back and listened intently so as not to miss any part of this mystical conversation.

The Cliff said to the Island, "Our dear child, are you now happy that you have finally been separated from us? Do you now feel as though all your burdens have been lifted, since you are now free? We see you in the distance, tall and strong, and we feel a sense of pride and sadness. You are a part of us. Under this water, you share the same roots as us. Yet above the water, you stand tall on your own to face your destiny by yourself. All we wish to know is that you are indeed happy."

The Island replied, "O Mother and Father, I am happy to be on my own and to enjoy my own freedom. I was happy when I was with you, but it was a different type of happiness. It was the happiness that a child enjoys as it grows with its parents. And now that I am on my own, I enjoy a different form of happiness that stems from my freedom. It is not as if I was unhappy being with you. I just enjoy this different sense of freedom. At my feet, I still share the same roots as you and this bond we shall have together forever. So, do not be sad that I am away from you, for indeed, I am never away from you. The rock at the bed of the Ocean bears witness to this."

The Cliff then said, "We worry about you as we watch the waves come crashing against you. You are exposed to these waves from all sides, for there is nothing to protect you. These waves will wear you down, our dear child. This is what makes us sad."

The Island then said, "My dear Parents, you are indeed right. I am exposed to the waves on all sides. Look at you! You only face the waves on one side for the rest of you is protected by the land that lies behind you. This is the land of our ancestors. You will wear down a lot slower than I will. But you must not be sad for me. I have chosen a path that is different. For this, I will meet an end that is different from yours — no better or no worse."

The Cliff replied, "We stayed as part of our ancestors. This has kept us alive and protected for this long. Yes, the waves will wear us down one day, but we will have the benefit of enjoying our lives under this protection of our ancestors for much longer than you will! This, O Beloved child, is what makes us grieve for you. Yet, we are also proud to watch you stand so tall and strong by yourself."

The Island then said, "You see, Life is not necessarily the passage of time. If you measure Life as purely a passage of time, then indeed I may have done the wrong thing by breaking away from you, for I could have been around for much longer had I stayed as a part of you and the protective land of my ancestors. I too, would only wear down from one side because of the waves, while the rest of me would remain protected. To me, Life is much more than just the passage of time. I broke loose to stand on my own because I sought "experience." This "experience" will come to me as I stand by myself and the price I pay will be my rapid ageing due to the waves. We all do age because the waves hit us all the time. You are just going to age slower than me. But ultimately, our final ending will be the same."

The Cliff then said, "We understand your thoughts. You are right in saying that Life is not a mere passage of time, but rather, it is a process of acquiring Knowledge and experience. But you are so dear to us and we see you wear away in front of us so fast that it makes us grieve. No parents can bear the thought of watching their child wither away in front of them even though they may be proud of the courage and strength that the child shows during this most painful process."

The Island seemed to smile as it said, "My dear Parents, I have already learned so much in the short time that I have been away from you. Indeed, I feel the pain as the waves carve away at my body. But, as each piece of me is carved away, it is carried by the Ocean to many distant lands. You don't even realize that since I broke away from you, the waves have carried so many small fragments of me back to you where I happily cling to your bosom. You are so distraught at watching me that you do not realize the little miracles that have occurred around you! There are so many parts of me that are back with you. Must we not be grateful for that? Then, there are parts of me that are being carried away to distant lands where I cling to new cliffs and become a member of other families whose ancestors protect them. Some parts of me become pure white sand that adds colour and beauty to the distant beaches. There was even a part of me that was washed to a place where fragments from other rocks began to cling to me and I have begun to grow. As more of them cling to me, I will grow into a new land, and I will indeed become the ancestor to others of my offspring.

"My beloved Parents, you too are part of me as I become an ancestor to others. You and I are connected by the land that lies under us. We have the same roots. Well, we also are connected by the same land to the new part of me that is growing into a new Island on the other side of the world. The roots are the same; it is just a matter of greater distance. You see, as our time shrinks, the distances just grow. We never cease to be because a small part of us is carried everywhere by the Ocean. So, my beloved Parents, when one day you look out and see me no more, do not grieve for me because I truly haven't left you. I am a part of you and I am a part of all the land that lies under the Ocean, and the land that lies above the Ocean. In some distant place, I have become a new Island. I have become an ancestor to others. Therefore, to me there is no end, for there never really was a beginning. The only part of me that began was at the Command of the Origin. This is the part of me that is Eternal. Our Forms will come and go. We may separate through time and distance. But we are indeed always One. We are always a part of each other. So, my dear Parents, do not say goodbye to me when I am gone, for I have never really left you."

The Cliff wept as it said, "Our dear child, you are indeed full of wisdom. All this time, small fragments of us have been carried away to distant lands, but we never truly realized this. There are new Islands growing out there that we are a part of, just as you are. We are part of a much greater family, but we never realized it until this moment. After you are gone, parts of us will continue to travel in the waves and we will mingle into one another in so many distant places. For this wonderful blessing of being Eternal, we thank our Origin. You are right, O beloved child, we are all Eternal from the moment of our Creation. It took your breaking away from us to teach us this lesson. We were so engrossed in you that we failed to realize the greater reality of Life. It is much greater than the passage of time or distance. Our dear child, it took your breaking away for us to realize the truth about ourselves. You know, although you may wither away much faster, your Knowledge transcends the shortness of your time in this single physical form that we see. Indeed, O beloved child, the truth is that you are our Parent, not our Child!"

Received on June 17, 1995.

May we learn to see and appreciate our children in the correct light. May we learn to see and appreciate our parents accordingly.

For those of us whose children are sick or terminally ill, may we learn to see the greater dimension of their lives through the words of the Island.

For those of us who have lost our loved ones through death, may the story of the Cliff and the Island help us to understand that our loved ones have never truly left us.

For those of us who are parents that cling too tightly to our children, may we learn to let go, for they have a right to their own destiny. May we learn to accept that it is possible for our children to possess greater wisdom than we do.

TWENTY-THREE

THE *C*HILD IN THE *R*OSE

It was eleven months ago that I was presented with a Rose and received Her message as revealed to you in Chapter 2.

Today, again, I am presented with a beautiful rose. It is not a tightly closed bud, and neither is it a fully opened flower. I hold this dainty rose in front of me and look directly into its apex. I see reams and reams of neatly tucked petals, all arranged in an enchanting array of little circles. And, as I look into the centre of the bud, the circles become smaller and tighter.

The rosebud then says to me, *"Amyn, I am like a little child. In me, in my core, you have seen rings and rings of petals, whose full form is not visible as yet. You know that these petals are eagerly waiting to open up into a fully blossomed flower.*

Then you will be able to see the true colour and shade of each and every petal."

Children are like rosebuds, clearly shaped with rings and rings of petals that we can identify, but not see fully. Hence we can only but try to imagine what a child will turn out to be as he or she grows up. Children must be allowed to grow, *gradually*. They need to be nourished. Parents are like the branches or stems of the rosebush. The strength of the stem determines the stability of the bud.

Let each petal in the rosebud open slowly and gently, so that it may reveal its precious beauty to the eyes of the beholder. Each petal in the bud is like a hidden secret in itself. It can only be revealed when the bud is ready to open. If you open up the bud too soon, these beautiful petals will be blown away by the wind. Allow Mother Nature to take Her course. Let each child blossom in its own way, for when a bud blossoms on its own, the flower always turns out to be healthy, strong and pretty. Never rush Nature. Do not *rush* the development of your child, for if you cannot be patient enough to wait for the bud to open naturally, you risk losing the bud itself and the flower to be.

Remember, the children in our lives come from the Origin. We do not have any control over their birth, life or death. The Origin does. Throughout the course of history, humanity has raised children through the process of intervention. This intervention has governed to a large extent the character and strength of children. Nature, my dear friends, does not proceed by intervention. On the contrary, Nature relies on evolution. As parents, we must be firm and strong stems for our children to thrive on. We must give them all the best that we can. But in doing so, we must not *intervene* in our child's development. Remember, Nature is where the child originates from, not from us! We must follow the laws of Nature in the development of our children. Remember, *evolution* is the key, not *intervention*. And when in doubt we must remember the rosebud's advice: *"You are the stem and not the Gardener — So, Let it Be!"*

Received on September 30, 1994.

TWENTY-FOUR

THE *M*ESSAGE OF *W*ISDOM: THE JOURNEY OF LIFE

It was early morning when we boarded the old, four-masted sailing ship at the port of Tangier in Morocco. It looked at least one hundred years old as it floated silently and majestically in the calm Mediterranean waters. There was a sense of complete serenity. I felt secure as I sat on an old wooden bench on the deck. This will be a good journey, I thought. I looked at the horizon and saw what looked like a huge mass of water that had calmly gone to sleep. Even the tiniest ripples that were caused by the blowing of the gentle winds were clearly visible. These ripples could never shake up a sailing ship like ours, I thought to myself. Our destination was Algiers. I thought of the people that awaited me in Algiers. I was excited about this journey.

At 7:30 a.m. we set sail. I waved goodbye to some little children that stood at the harbour. Their little hands swayed from side to side as they waved us goodbye. The innocence in their eyes told me that they genuinely prayed for our safe journey. We drifted away slowly towards the horizon, led gently by the calm winds. I was now in the hands of the Wind. Before I boarded this ship, I was in control of where I went, for all I depended upon was my feet to carry me. But now I was in the hands of the Wind. Yes, the Sails had some influence on our direction, but we were no longer in control. I started to feel a long and distant sense of helplessness. Somehow, now, I was going to be led into the deep blue Ocean by a Wind that I could neither see, nor govern. But sure as daylight, it was there to carry me on my journey.

I then heard the Divine Voice say to me, *"You are now on your journey. You have left the shores of security and ventured into the Ocean, where insecurity surrounds you everywhere. You are being carried by the invisible Wind, whom you know not, and whom you understand not! Yet you have placed yourself in its hands! When you boarded this ship, the Wind was so calm that you never stopped for a moment to think. The calmness gave you a sense of security. And yet, now this very Wind surrounds you with insecurity. But you cannot turn back for the ship has set sail. From here, you can either sink, reach your destination, or reach a destination that you know not! Those are the choices. And if you should jump off this ship,*

*there are sharks around you that will devour you.
You boarded this ship in the first place because
you had a purpose, which was to travel to Algiers.
For this purpose, you traded the security of the
shores for the insecurity of the Ocean. You took
yourself from a position of control and placed
yourself in the hands of the Winds that you can
neither see nor predict.*

*"Now think carefully, Amyn, about how you must
proceed on this journey. Firstly, you must forget the
security of the shore, because it no longer exists.
Hence, do not use it as a reference point for
making any decisions. If you forget the security of
the shores, then you will indeed not sense or feel
the insecurity of the Ocean; for if there is no
concept of security in your mind, then the concept
of insecurity also fails to exist.*

*"Set your sights very clearly on Algiers. Set
your Compass to accurately face Algiers. Now, use
the steady direction of the Compass as your guide.
Steer your way so that the needle of the Compass
is always constantly facing Algiers. In other words,
My Beloved One, be flexible in your steering, but
firm in your direction. The moment you let the
Compass waver, you will lose your direction. And
then it will be very difficult to find your way for you
are in the hands of the invisible Wind. And when
you enter the storm and the Waves come crashing
against your ship, you will find it more difficult to
keep your Compass pointed steadily at Algiers. At*

this time you must be even more flexible than ever before.

"Remember that the Waves of the Ocean are your best friend and they can also be your worst enemy. Do not be guided by them, for despite the fact that they are fully visible to you, they can lead you towards the unknown. On the other hand, the Wind that you do not see is more your friend than the Waves that you do see. Guide your Sails by making friends with the Wind. Do not look at each big wave come at you, for no sooner has one passed, there will be another! You can never stop that for it is the law of the Ocean. Do not try to fight the Waves for you will tire. And when you find yourself looking too much at the Waves, take a break and go back to the Compass. Realize that you must never take your eyes off the Compass. You must always look towards Algiers and draw strength from the Compass for it is your sure guide. The Waves will smash against your boat. When one hits hard at the boat, you will fear that the next one will make you sink. In that fear, you will no longer see the Compass for you have shifted your mind from the sure direction to the unsure speculation of the end, that may or may not come.

"Remember, on this journey, Amyn, there is no end. If you should fail to reach Algiers, you will keep coming back again and again, and braving Ocean upon Ocean until you get to Algiers. If this is the truth about Life, then why do you let the Waves and the storms take you away from your destination? For each storm that takes you off course, you will have to come back and brave ten more storms in order to get back on course.

"I give you this Message as the Message of Wisdom, for staying on course is the Path of Wisdom.

"Keeping your eyes keenly focused on Algiers is the Path of the Exalted.

"Believing in the Compass is the Path of Faith.

"And last but not least, steering your way through the Ocean, the Waves, the storms and the Winds, carve out for you the Path of Destiny. Set your eyes on the Exalted and Destiny is yours, for Life is an Exalted Destiny!

"Have Faith and be firm in your trust in the Origin, and your Compass will never waver.

"Remember that the Wind that you do not see is your friend. The Wind is the energy that leads you along the Exalted Destiny. Harness this 'Energy' very carefully.

"In Life, wealth is like the Wind. It can be your best friend if you harness it carefully. Intelligence is also like the Wind. But try not to wrap your arms around the Wind to keep it forever, because it never was yours and never will be yours. Chasing high Winds leads you to storms that could sink you. Be smart and 'use' the Wind to propel you on the Exalted Destiny. This Wind is for all to use. But, Wind alone, and its careful management, does not get you to Algiers. It takes a lot more. In Life, wealth and intelligence can be your friends, if you 'use' them correctly. Do not try to own them, for 'he who tries to catch the Wind is the fool of the day'.

"When your ship slows down because the Wind is dying out, do not desperately search for the Wind, for it is not there to be found. But rather, change the direction of the Sails and 'use' the Waves, which I said to you earlier could be your enemy or your friend. Align your Sails to take advantage of the Waves and cruise gently until the Wind and you can be back together again. But keep your eyes on Algiers and the Compass at all times. After all, by doing so, you are still on the path of Destiny. And remember, Wisdom is essential in all you do. But this Wisdom must be applied to yourself, the Winds, the Waves, the Compass and your Sails. Each decision you take must draw from the Wisdom that resides within you. Your Faith and Trust in your Origin, with your eyes fixed upon the Path of the Exalted, will yield the deepest, innermost Wisdom from within you, that will keep all the elements of your journey in 'Balance'. Sadness and happiness in Life are like the Waves — one follows the other. Make the Waves your friend and you will be happy. Make them your enemy and you will be sad.

"In the name of the Origin, you will reach Algiers, for that is to Be. Read My Message carefully, and then meditate over it. Base all your decisions in Life on this Message, for I have called it the Message of Wisdom for good reason. Remember, in Life, when troubles hit you one after another, do not have any fear. Stop to realize that you have shifted your eyesight from the Compass to the Waves. Go back to the Compass and look out at Algiers and you will get back on track again.

"Then, one morning will come when you will look towards Algiers and begin to see the shoreline that you had so anxiously awaited. This is the shoreline that will bring back security to you again. Then, stop and ask yourself, 'Has this journey made me any Wiser?' If the answer is No, then the shoreline you are looking at may not be Algiers!"

Received on March 3, 1995.

My dear friends,

May we learn to live our lives with the help of the Message of Wisdom. In this beautiful Chapter lie the answers and solutions to all the problems and crises that we may face in our daily lives, no matter how small or how large they may be. Let us thank the Origin for blessing us with this Very Special Message.

TWENTY-FIVE

"Now:"

YOUR MOST BEAUTIFUL MOMENT

My dear friends, it is my honour to share with you this special Revelation on the importance of Now, or the Present. Every Choice in the Present creates the Future and becomes the Past. In this Revelation we will also learn about "Karma," which is a Universal Law that says, "Every deed or action will be met by a corresponding reaction from within the Universe." This Law forms the origin of the statement, "Thou shall reap what thou sows."

I hear the Divine Voice say, *"Write about the important aspect of Life, which calls for living in the Present. From birth to death, every creature experiences sequences of events which lead it from a set beginning to a particular ending. Destiny* indeed does exist. However, the direction of one's Life is a combination of Choice and Destiny. This is indeed very true for the Creation of Higher Intellect.

"Life is a series of Crossroads. At each Crossroad, one has to decide whether to turn right, left or to go straight ahead or to go backwards. The selection of the direction determines what Crossroad one will face next. Each Choice carves the course of one's Life. Each Choice governs one's Destiny. Destiny provides for the Crossroad itself. It makes the Crossroad available. However, Choice is the important element that guides one's Destiny. When one's Life begins, a goal is set for what the Soul must achieve during the Lifetime. Yet one's deeds, actions and Choices clearly govern whether this goal is accomplished or not.

"The Law of Karma, which says that 'Every deed or action will be met by a corresponding reaction from within the Universe', can be clearly explained through the aspects of Destiny and Choice, for Choice governs Karma. There are Souls that positively advance in their journey through correct Choices that are made in their physical manifestation. There are others that remain stagnant and then there are many that actually regress or go backwards. Where then does Faith fit into this multitude of aspects? Keeping or having Faith in the Origin and following the Statement of Universal Truth, which says, 'I am You and You are Me and Together We are Everything', leads one to make correct Choices. Those who constantly search for the Light of the Origin and live by the Statement of Universal Truth will be blessed with the Divine Guidance which will help to ensure that the correct Choices are made at all times. This will lead to the Highest of Endings. People who are graced with the Divine Guidance are prevented from doing the wrong thing or exercising the wrong Choices by the creation of circumstances that force the Correct Choice. Therefore it is very important for each being to understand the aspects of Crossroads, Destiny, Choice, Karma, Faith and Divine Guidance. This understanding will help to provide a balanced framework through which one can lead one's Life. These aspects may seem complex but they are rather simple indeed.

"When We use the term Ending, it does not imply that death is actually the end. Death is simply the point where the physical form comes to its conclusion. The journey of the Soul is Eternal. In this regard, the journey of the Soul through a given Lifetime can be compared to the climbing of a staircase. The question at birth is, 'How many steps can you climb through this Lifetime?' The question at death is, 'How many steps did you climb through this Lifetime?' In these words of wisdom are important elements for humanity to learn from. Write about how one must never forsake the Present for the Past or the Future."

I am but a simple human being and all I can write about is a "state of mind" that we need to achieve in order to create harmony between the aspects of Crossroads, Destiny, Choice, Karma, Faith and Divine Guidance.

My dear friends, let us think about the concept of "NOW." What is "NOW"? What is the "Present"? How can our understanding and management of Now enable us to rapidly ascend the Staircase of Life? Life itself is a sequence of events. Do you realize that every moment that goes by becomes part of the total History of the Universe? Therefore the Past is very long indeed! Every action that you take instantly becomes part of the Past, which is recorded in the History of the Universe.

Take the simple example of drinking a glass of water:

There is a moment in the sequence of events when you fill the glass and then bring it to your lips and then drink it.

In the History of the Universe, a glass was filled.

The next event recorded is that the glass was brought to your lips.

Following that, the next event recorded was the fact that the water was drunk.

Yet, when you originally lifted the glass to fill it, the Future would have stated that water was going to enter the glass.

Once the glass was full, the Past recorded the full glass but the Future now stated that the glass would reach your lips.

Once this had happened, History recorded that the glass had reached your lips.

But now the Future stated that the water would be drunk and when this had occurred, History recorded the fact accordingly.

Can you see how the Past and Future almost flow into one another? *Yet there is a very, very fine line that separates the Past and the Future, which is the Present or Now.* How long is the Present? One can argue that it is a day long, or an hour long, or a second long or a microsecond long. Or does it almost not exist? You can see that the Present is a lot, lot shorter than the Past or the Future. Yet it is the Present that causes the Past to record the event, and it is the Present that dictates the direction that the Future will take.

Think about the glass of water once more:

The Future stated that the glass would be filled.

Once full, it became an event of the Past.

Then, the Future stated that you would bring the glass to your lips in order to drink the water. But if in that Present moment you chose to pour the water out of the glass rather than bring it to your lips, then you would have clearly changed the Future!

The Future will now state that you will put the glass back on the shelf rather than bring it to your lips! In this small example, you can see how the Present, short as it may be, totally influences the Past and the Future.

My dear friends, in living your lives, I urge you to learn to respect the Present, for it is one of the most important aspects of Living. The Present governs everything. Yet it is so sad to see people lose the Present because they are so worried about the Future! They must realize that the Present actually governs the Future! Then there are people who lose the Present because they live in the memories of the Past. They must realize that the Past is purely a product of what the Present was at some given point in time. My advice to you is to live the Present fully and correctly. Use every bit of the Present (which is so short that it almost does not exist) to help you to rapidly ascend the Staircase of Life.

Let us come back to the Crossroads again:

In the context of what I have just said, the Past represents the Crossroads that have gone by. One must learn from them.

The Future represents the Crossroad that you are approaching.

The Present represents when you are at the Crossroad itself.

The Present is the only time when you can exercise your Choice. This Choice will lead you to the next Crossroad.

Of course, your Choice will be governed or influenced by the Crossroads and experiences of the Past, plus the application of the Ethics that come from your Faith and the Statement of Universal Truth. If you seek help from your Origin, you will also be guided at each Crossroad towards making the Correct Choice. It is this Choice that will determine your Future. Hence I urge you to recognize the importance of Now or the Present. Do not lose it to the Past with no gain. When you write the word NOW backwards, it reads WON. Capture NOW and your battle will be WON!

Received on September 24, 1995.

TWENTY-SIX

*A*BORTION:

CHOICES AND CONSEQUENCES

My dear friends, please read this Chapter in conjunction with the previous Chapter entitled *Now: Your Most Beautiful Moment* for they are closely inter-related.

I hear the Divine Voice say, *"Amyn, talk about Choice from the perspective of the issues that plague so many people in their daily lives. Use an example of Abortion, which is a matter of great controversy. Apply in simple terms the aspects of Crossroads, Destiny, Choice, Karma, Faith and Divine Guidance to this very controversial matter. Through your explanation, those that understand may learn to apply these aspects to all other*

*issues and challenges in their lives, no matter how
sensitive these issues may be."*

My dear friends, I have been directed by the Origin to
share with you special inspirations on the subject of
Abortion, with particular reference to the application of
Choice. From all the Chapters of this book, we have
learned that the Creation of Life itself is most sacrosanct
and Divine. The Chapters 12 and 13 on *The Bubble: Five
Ways to Break Free* and *The Revelation on Pregnancy,*
illustrate this aspect very clearly. These chapters talk
about the spiritual dimension of sex and conception. In
the light of this spiritual understanding, the issue of
Abortion becomes a very grave matter indeed. During
the process of sexual intercourse, there comes about a
Union of two bodies and two Souls. This spiritual Union
occurs in the presence of the Light of the Origin, which
results in the granting of the new Soul of the child
within the Soul of the mother. This bond has been
created within the Highest Spiritual Order, and its
destruction through Abortion could have devastating
consequences from a spiritual perspective.

However, as beings of Higher Intellect, we have been
bestowed with the ability to make Choices, even if these
Choices could bring about the greatest of material and
spiritual catastrophes. Therefore, a couple that is faced
with the option of an Abortion has a Choice to make, and

the respective consequences to face. My dear friends, the following parable provides invaluable insights into the issue of Abortion.

There was once a very happy family that lived in New Mexico. There was a father, mother and a daughter who shared a very close and loving relationship. The daughter's name was Claire. She was sixteen years old and was growing into a beautiful young lady. Her mother, Sally, had taken great pains to explain to Claire the facts of life, sex, children, moral and religious values. They were a devout Christian family. Claire had a boyfriend whose name was Sam. He was eighteen years old and came from a broken family. His parents were divorced when he was only three years old. He grew up with his father, Richard, who was too busy developing his law practice. For his 18th birthday, Richard had bought Sam a new Lexus automobile.

One Saturday evening, Sam picked up Claire at 7:00 p.m. to go out on a date with her. Here was a young couple, bursting with life and energy! They drove to a quiet, private spot and parked under a tree. It was getting dark. They held each other tight in an embrace. They were in love. Sam proceeded to try and seduce Claire into having intercourse with him. When things had gone far enough, Claire suddenly realized that it had to stop. She could not go through with this — it was wrong! Yet Sam could hardly be stopped! What followed was a great argument because Sam felt that Claire was being unfair. The intercourse did not occur.

Sam drove off in a rage and they did not talk to each other practically all evening. After dinner, they stopped at a bar for a drink. By this time both of them had calmed down and they made up over their gins and tonics. The drinking continued and by the time they left the bar, Sam was in no condition to even walk, let alone drive. They got into the Lexus and headed towards Claire's home. Sam drove at a speed of 80 m.p.h. in a 30 m.p.h. zone over the mountains. He turned a sharp bend and lost control. The car left the road and rolled over several times. Neither of them was wearing a seat belt and they were both flung into the back seat. The car finally came to a standstill at the edge of a steep cliff. The front wheels had rolled off the edge and the car hung there, pivoting. Any pressure toward the front would send the car three thousand feet down into the valley.

When Sam and Claire came back to their senses, it was early morning. They found themselves sitting in the back seat of the wrecked Lexus. As Sam moved, the car began to tilt downwards! They realized that the end was close. Claire tried to open the rear door but it had seized shut as a result of the roll-over. Sam's door was in the same condition. How could they get out? In the distance thunderclouds had begun to gather. It appeared certain that the storm and rain would push the Lexus over the cliff. Sam and Claire had to get out. The only way was to climb over to the front seat and exit from the passenger-side door, which was partially open. As Claire tried to climb towards the front seat, the car tilted sharply forward. She could not do it! Sam tried too, with no luck. They had come dangerously close to going over the cliff.

While Sam and Claire tried to work through their crisis in the midst of a severe hangover, an elderly couple, Peter and Sarah, came cycling up the mountain for their early morning exercise. They stopped at the wrecked Lexus and were terrified to see these two lovely children who were about to plunge to their deaths. Peter began to panic and kept yelling to Sam and Claire to remain still and not to move. But what Choice did the poor kids have? The storm had started to rage and the car was rocking gently in the wind.

Just then, Michael, who was a mechanic, drove by and stopped when he saw what had happened. He grabbed his tools and rushed over to the Lexus. He tried to pry open the rear door with no luck. The rear window was also not an option since the roof had caved in. He did not have too many Choices. That rear door had to be opened very soon. He found a long piece of wood which he tried to wedge into the rear door like a crowbar, in an attempt to force the door open. He had to push hard on his makeshift crowbar. He gave it a heave and the car began to roll forward. Peter, panic-stricken, ordered Michael to stop. "You will kill them!" he yelled at Michael.

To that Michael replied, "I have to get them out or they are dead anyways!" With that, he gave the crowbar another heave and the car started to tilt sharply forward. Peter rushed over and grabbed Michael to stop him from pushing the door any further. What followed was a struggle between Peter and Michael. In desperation Peter hit Michael over the head with a rock and knocked him unconscious! Michael started to bleed from his nose and ears. The storm was now in full swing. Peter was in a state of serious panic and Sarah was hysterical. In the midst of this chaos, Sam looked into Claire's eyes and said, "We have to do something. We have to make a Choice! What is it going to be? Claire, my darling, should we try the front door one more time?"

Claire quietly replied, "We can wait here to be rescued but the storm will take us down. If we climb over to the front, the car will go down the cliff! What is our Choice, Sam?"

They paused for a moment and then said to each other, "Let's go for the front door!" As Peter saw this, he screamed to them to sit still and not to move. But Claire and Sam had made their Choice. As Claire climbed over into the front seat, there was a huge creak and the Lexus went right over the cliff. It burst into flames as it hit the ground. Then there was a huge explosion and it was all over. Sam and Claire were no more. They were claimed into History. Peter knelt down and cried. Michael lay there in a pool of blood. It was all over.

In this simple story lie so many answers. First, earlier in the evening, Claire exercised her Choice by stopping Sam from having intercourse with her. Based upon her upbringing, this was the correct thing to do. Sam was enraged because his Choice had not been honoured. As they drank in the bar, Claire was uncomfortable because she felt that they had had too much to drink. She even volunteered to call her father to pick them up. This infuriated Sam and Claire chose to be quiet and not to push her luck any further with Sam. Then as Sam drove at high speeds, for that was his Choice, Claire kept pleading with him to slow down. But it was to no avail. Then came the accident! The mistake had been made! Here sat two lovely children at the edge of death. Whatever Choice they made would have drastic consequences. Then came along Peter and Sarah. Peter kept telling the children what to do, and yet, he could not really do anything to help them! It was easy for Peter, standing away from the forsaken car, to tell Sam and Claire what they should do! He tried to influence their Choice by imposing his Choice upon them. Then came along Michael, the mechanic, who tried to help Sam and Claire, but in doing so, he also added to their peril! When Peter grabbed Michael and hit him over the head with a rock, he did something that he had no right to do! His actions did not help Claire and Sam in any way. In fact, had he not intervened, Michael may have saved them. Or, it is also possible that Michael may have sent them down the cliff sooner! Who knows?

My dear friends, take a look at a young couple that is faced with the Choice of an Abortion. They have made their first mistake by engaging in sexual intercourse irresponsibly, without adequate understanding of their actions or without the use of adequate protection. Their Choice has led to the pregnancy. They are like Sam and Claire with the car tilting over the cliff. Then there are people who denounce Abortion and even become violent about it! Can you see Peter in that picture? It is easy for anti-abortionists to condemn what is happening and try to tear down the clinics. That's what Peter did. Abortion doctors have been shot at and attacked. In some ways, Michael the mechanic would understand the predicament of the doctors!

When the couple makes their Choice to go ahead with an Abortion, the consequences may be far worse than going down a cliff. But they are the ones in the car at the edge of the cliff, and they have the right to make their Choice, whether it be right or wrong. Sam and Claire made their Choice, which led them to their death.

You can see how Sam reached his Crossroads and made his Choices. Claire also reached her Crossroads and made her Choices. The net result was a disaster. Peter, who thought he was doing the right thing, ended up doing the wrong thing. Michael was trained as a mechanic and he only did what he knew best.

My dear friends, every being has the right to make his or her own Choices. In fact, the very dignity of a being stems from this right to Choose. Every Choice has a Consequence. In the story of Sam and Claire lie important answers and guidelines on how we make our decisions in life. Never impose your Choice on others for

that takes away their Dignity. Never judge others for the
Origin is the only true judge of all. By all means, we
must help those in need of help. In the case of Abortion,
the correct solution lies in *educating* children in a
manner whereby they can be helped to make their
Choices correctly. Rather than publicly demonstrate
against something, it is better to spend your time
making your life and your actions exemplary for those
who you want to try and help. When you feel the urge to
condemn and protest, remember Sam and Claire. *They*
are the ones in the car at the edge of their death. Help
them and help prevent the Sams and Claires of tomorrow
by promoting education from schools down to the very
core of every family. While this is no easy task, it must
be done. The price of failure is way too high!

Received On September 24, 1995.

*May we learn valuable lessons from the parable
of Sam and Claire. May we learn to understand
the importance of making correct choices. May
we learn to recognize that the solution to Abortion
lies in education, at the school and family level. It
is not a matter for governments and lawmakers to
legislate or pass judgement upon, for the Choices
and Consequences are of a very personal nature*

indeed. May we try our best to help prevent the tragedies of the Sams and Claires of tomorrow, through prayer, Love, compassion, understanding and education.

THE ORIGIN OF THE EARTH

To celebrate our wedding anniversary on August 7, 1994, my wife Karima, the children and I took a fishing trip in Thailand, off the coast of Phuket. As the boat left the shore, I said to my family, "Twelve years ago today, your mother and I were married and we started a new Life together. We have shared this Life in the Garden of the Origin. In this Garden, we have been blessed with four flowers that we have looked after — Adil, Aly, Raheena, and Noorin. And in this Garden we have been very happy with our greater family, which includes all our fellow beings, the Earth, the Ocean, the Skies, the Sun, the Stars and the Universe."

This being such a special day for us, we decided to spend it with Mother Ocean. As we went deeper into the Indian Ocean, I began to think about the origins of Life.

I asked Mother Ocean to share with me the secrets of how Life came about on this Earth. Here is the beautiful story that She had to tell:

"In the Universe, there are Stars, Planets, Moons, the Sun, bodies of matter, and numerous forces that you cannot comprehend. At one point, a small fraction of the Sun was ordained to break away from its Parent. This was part of the Origin's Continuous Creation. This little fraction was to become the Earth. And, like the Earth, there were other fractions that also parted from the Sun. The Universe is the sum total of fractions, whose limits are infinite."

The Ocean continued: *"The Sun said to its beloved fraction (the Earth), 'You are leaving Me, your home, to become a home in yourself to other Creations of the Origin. You and I are One and together, we are One with the Universe. When you leave Me, you take a part of Me with you and this is the secret behind all the forms of Life that have been Created by the Origin of All Things. At this point in The Divine Will, every part of the Universe and every form of Life that is Created grows and spreads by dividing itself, and each new part carries the Essence of its predecessor. All forms of Life that you will become home to will follow this process. But remember, My dear, that there will come a time when by the Divine Will all fractions will begin to come together again into one Total Union. Therefore, My dear, you leave Me today and you travel far away from Me, but there will reach a point when you will start to come back to Me. You will always be nurtured by Me. All Life that exists within you will be nurtured by Me. I will give to you everything that you need; for you and I are both parts of the Origin, the Giver of All Things. The further away from Me that you travel, the more difficult it will be for you. Disintegration will occur within yourself. But there will come a point in time when you will move away no further. You will start to come back closer to Me, until you will finally merge into Me once again.'"*

The Ocean continued: *"As the Earth moved away from the Sun, it began to spin on its own and with distance, it became a 'ball of fire' as you call it. In fact, it was not quite a 'ball of fire'. It carried within it a part of the Sun, which represented a form of Energy which then transformed itself into Matter. But My definition of Energy and Matter are not the same as what your science has taught you. Your understanding of Energy is at a very rudimentary level, where you take fuel in the form of matter and convert it into heat, electricity, power, etc. This conversion is a very primitive practice. The day your science discovers how to transform Matter into Energy in the form that I am referring to, your world will change dramatically, and the Earth may no longer be able to sustain any life forms."*

The Ocean then said, *"When the Energy converted itself into Matter, water was the key by-product of this process. This is why I say that in water lies immense Energy. At the beginning, the entire Earth was covered with water. The land mass, which was also a product of this Energy-to-Matter conversion, was fully covered by water. The Ocean picked up salt from the land below it. Then, by the Will of the Origin, there were life forms created in the water. This was followed by a redistribution of water. There was evaporation of water from the Ocean and further redistribution occurred through the clouds. Hence, the level of the Ocean fell, and its depths also changed due to gravitational effects. The land under the Ocean began to surface in various places. Then lakes and rivers were formed through this process of redistribution of fresh water. This is why all lakes and rivers ultimately return or drain back into the Ocean. The life forms in the Ocean that ended up on the land went through a process of evolution, from fish to amphibians to mammals, birds, reptiles, etc. The human respiratory system can be traced back to the gills in fish. Of course, you consumed fresh water that collected on the land, and that is how your life cycles evolved and developed."*

Today, it is very clear to me how all this happened. The day before I spoke to the Ocean I had really no idea or opinion on the Origins of the Earth.

I have now also realized that the reason the salt content in the Ocean remains constant is that there is a fixed total amount of water on this planet. It just keeps getting redistributed. For the longest time I have meditated on how Oceans became salty in the first place and what really happened. Now I have my answer. The saltwater has always been there from the time of the Earth's formation. Fresh water came from the redistribution process.

The Ocean also told me to take a hard look at the water molecule if I wanted to remove salt from water. By pursuing this avenue of thought we can and will find a way to remove salt from water and in the process release vast quantities of Energy. I know that in time, we will be shown how to achieve this. We do not really need oil and other pollution-causing energy sources. I believe that through this discovery will come a dramatic reduction in the pollution of the Earth — remember what the Sun said, *"The further away from Me you go, the more you will disintegrate within yourself. But, when you turn around and start coming back to Me, you will heal."* We have damaged our environment. It is time for Healing and the change for the good has begun! Hence, we will discover a greater source of Energy in water, which we can utilize in harmony with the Earth.

After receiving what the Ocean had to share with me, I have come to believe that we have misunderstood the Sun. It is not a ball of fire! It has the same shape as the Earth, the planets, and all other bodies or fragments that surround it. (A good analogy is the common genes that we find between parents and children.) The Sun said to the Earth when they parted, *"My Love will always surround you and nurture you and all Life that you will become home to."*

This Love of the Sun is an Energy that manifests itself in different forms. For creatures on the Earth, it manifests itself as light and heat. But, that does not make the Sun a ball of fire — in thinking so, we are naive! I am not an astronomer and know little about outer space, but, as we travel away from the Earth into space, it does not necessarily get "hotter." Why? Think about it. This is where the Esoteric aspects of Life begin to explain to us what is going on. The Love from the Sun is an Energy that manifests itself differently in these "Homes of Life Forms" like the Earth. It may not always take the form of heat or light. In the same way, the Stars are not distant balls of fire. The Stars are part of the Universe that carry a special form of Energy, Knowledge and Love in themselves.

My dear friends, the Earth has begun to turn back and go towards the Sun. I learned from the Ocean that the year 2000 AD marks a significant period in this process of reversal. This is why I say that evil has bottomed out and the tide of good has begun — because we have stopped moving away from the Sun and are now moving back towards It!

Received on August 13, 1994.

I pray that we may derive a special understanding from the beautiful Message that the Ocean has shared with us. May this shape our outlook towards our precious home, the Earth, and its All-Giving parent, the Sun. As the Earth has started moving back to the Sun, I pray that we may draw upon all the positive energies of this special event and ride the crests of the waves of "good," for evil indeed has bottomed out. May this Knowledge fill our hearts and minds with Hope — for a better tomorrow.

TWENTY-EIGHT

THE $\mathscr{S}$TARS:

ASPECTS OF KNOWLEDGE

It is a dark night and I look into the sky at the thousands of little Stars that twinkle away in the distance. As I sit in the balcony of the condominium that we have rented at the Sheraton Hotel in Puerto Vallarta, Mexico, I hear the waves of the Ocean speak their words of wisdom as they reach the shore. The night is calm and I savour the wonderful atmosphere as I look into the dark Ocean and at all the lights that softly glimmer along Puerto Vallarta Bay. I have often wondered about the Stars and their role in the Universe. I have also prayed that the Origin may bless me with Knowledge pertaining to the Stars.

I look again into the dark sky and the Stars and ask, "What are the Stars? Why are they there in the sky?

What is their relationship to me? What is their role in the Universe? Are they little balls of fire out there in the galaxies as the scientists say? I pray, in the Name of the Origin, grant me the Knowledge of the Stars."

Then, above the sound of the Ocean waves, I hear the Divine Voice say, *"Amyn, the Stars are Aspects of Knowledge in the Universe. You perceive them with your human eyes as specks of light in the sky. They are not balls of fire that sit out there in open space! Remember, all Creation in the Universe has a purpose. Leaving balls of fire in suspension in space does not represent much of a purpose! All Our Creation in the Universe is linked together with a common Origin. Each aspect of Creation is closely interrelated to the others. The sum total of this interrelationship is the Origin, or what some may call Nature. The Stars, My dear Amyn, are not balls of fire in the sky. They are Aspects of Knowledge in the Universe.*

"In the Stars resides Knowledge of immense depth. This is a form of Knowledge that is difficult for the human mind to even start to perceive. If the brain in your head were like the Universe, then the various nerve endings that represent centres of Knowledge in the brain are synonymous with the Stars in the Universe. You can hardly call the nerve endings in your brain a galaxy comprised of balls of fire! In the same way, you must not take the naive interpretation of the Stars as being meaningless balls of fire in a galaxy in the sky.

"You asked the question about how human beings are related to the Stars. Well, each being is very closely related to the Stars, for the reservoir of Knowledge that resides within your Inner Self is no different to the Aspects of Knowledge that the Stars represent. The Knowledge of the Universe is like a Book containing an infinite number of pages. Each page represents the Knowledge of the Inner Self that resides within each being. This Knowledge is one of Totality, with all its multitude of Aspects. Each Aspect of this Knowledge is represented by a Star. All the Aspects combined with all the pages of the Book form the Knowledge of the Universe. You must then ask yourself as to what is the true distance between you and the Stars. The answer is very simple. You are as close to the Stars as you are to your Inner Self. For some beings, this places them extremely close to the Stars. Yet, for others, they are so far away from the Knowledge that resides within their Inner Selves that the Stars are almost completely out of reach.

"Each time you look at the Stars, remember the Book of the Universe. Remember that you are a page in that Book and, hence, you are inseparable from the Universe. Your characteristics in this material, physical form on Earth are indeed related to the Stars. When astrologers look at your Stars and tell you about yourself, all they are doing is recognizing certain Aspects about yourself that relate to the Aspects of certain Stars in the Book of the Universe. Astrology is a science and an art.

The true astrologer recognizes the esoteric relationship that exists between you and the Stars that are of closest impact to you. Once this relationship is identified, the astrologer is able to tell you about yourself for he or she can then read into some of the Aspects of you. Therefore, good astrologers are inspired beings who are gifted with these abilities. (Those who use these abilities for personal profit run the risk of losing this gift or collecting negative aspects that come from the abuse of this Knowledge.)

"However, it is most important to recognize that at a material plane, you can only read into the most superficial Aspects of Knowledge that relate you to the Stars. As you grow in your awareness of the Knowledge of the Universe, and as you begin to recognize the Knowledge that resides within your Inner Self, you will be able to clearly leaf through each page in the Book of the Universe. You will be closer to the Stars than the tip of your nose is to your face. At this point, all the Aspects of Knowledge that are represented in the Stars will begin to manifest in yourself. You will now be ready to receive the Knowledge of the Universe."

I asked the question, "What is an Aspect of Knowledge, O Divine Origin?"

I was then told, *"The concept of Aspects of Knowledge is difficult for your human mind to comprehend. You will need to draw on the Reservoir of Understanding that resides in your*

Inner Self to understand the meaning of Aspects of Knowledge. In an overly simplistic way, you may consider a prism through which you shine a beam of light. Call this the Mother beam. Before the Mother beam hits the prism, the light is a single, uniform beam. Yet, after it passes through the prism, it splits up into its component colours together with some degree of reflection and refraction. These component colours combined with the rays of reflection and refraction are synonymous with the Aspects of the Mother beam.

Now, a single prism can generate a certain combination of Aspects. If you were to pass the same Mother beam through a million prisms, consider what would happen! The Knowledge is like the Mother beam of light that enters the prisms. The Aspects of Knowledge are what you see coming out of the million prisms. And remember that all Components or Aspects that leave the prism are tightly interrelated to one another as well as to the Mother beam. The Stars, my dear Amyn, are like the Components of Knowledge as they leave a million prisms; but they are not truly Components because Components can be split apart. It is more accurate to describe them as Aspects because they cannot be split apart. They simply represent a set of Perspectives of the Mother beam. When you see the Stars all split up in the sky, do not for a moment believe that they are separate and distinct for if this were so, they

*would only be Components. They are indeed
closely interrelated, which makes them Aspects.*

*Remember, I told you that this was a very, very
simplistic view for your human mind to digest.
Consider this example as purely a seed of thought.
Now, meditate on this subject and this seed will
grow into a tree with an infinite number of
branches! This is how the understanding of the
Truth grows."*

To date in my life, I have always held a simplistic
view of our solar system and the Stars. Yet, with this
Revelation, I now see the role of the Stars as closely as I
can imagine the nerve centres in my brain. I pray to the
Origin, saying, "Thank you for granting me this
Knowledge."

I hear the Divine Voice say, *"Look at the human
body! How simple it is and yet how complex it is.
Scientists have spent lifetimes trying to learn about
the composition of this body. First, it was a macro-
level study. Then, it moved to the finer points and
today they are scratching the surface in terms of
the storage and expression of genetic information. I
say that they are scratching the surface because
the horse has not even stepped out of the stable,
let alone having started to run in the million-mile
race! But, Amyn, the human body with all its
intricacies does not come close to the Aspect of
Knowledge of one star! This is why I say to you that
the depth of this Knowledge is so vast that it is
beyond the capacity of the human mind to*

comprehend. It is your Inner Self that can help you receive and digest this Knowledge in its fullest form. The Stars that are closest to you in Aspect have a very interesting story to tell. No astrologer can read into this story. Just let things unfold before you and dig deep within yourself, for what you will find will be truly fulfilling. Encourage others to think about what has been said in this Chapter, for they too can gain immensely from trying to understand the Aspects of Knowledge. When they do, they will be like visitors in a garden full of Stars. This is a garden they will never want to leave!

Received on April 25, 1995.

TWENTY-NINE

$\mathscr{L}$AND FOR $\mathscr{S}$ALE

THE PROPHECY OF LOS ANGELES

On a dull, cloudy day I walked down one of the
busiest streets in Los Angeles. There were tall buildings
under construction. The names and credentials of the
contractors shone vividly from large signboards.
Vehicles passed by me, as did hundreds of people who
were oblivious to my presence. I then stopped at a
vacant site that lay in between the two tallest buildings
in the area. Some old building must have once stood on
this site. Of course, it had been demolished and all I
could see was the brown clay soil with the odd bricks
that remained from the building. I then noticed a
signpost which said, "Prime Downtown Lot for Sale."
As I looked at this lot, my mind began to flash back
thousands of years. There was a time when this very plot

lay at the bottom of the Ocean. Thousands of colourful fish swam around this lot, as did some large sharks. Of course, there were no buildings and there was no sign of the presence of people. It was all natural. In the distance, where the tallest building in Los Angeles stands today, were large coral rocks with sea vegetation of a multitude of colours. How beautiful! I thought. The Land under the sea seemed happy and content. It was home to millions of creatures of the Ocean that came and went from moment to moment.

I heard the rude hooting of a taxicab that brought me back to the present! It was not so beautiful any more! My eyes wandered back to the "Lot for Sale" sign. I looked at this plot of Land. It was barren and abused. I knelt down and picked up a fistful of dirt. As I brought the dirt closer to my eyes, I started to hear the sounds of a crying baby girl! She was hysterical and cried with a sound that represented the deepest form of sadness I have ever known. Around me I could see no baby, but the crying was loud and clear. At this point, I recognized that the dirt in my hand was where the sad sound was coming from. I paused for a moment and took a closer look at the dirt. "In the name of the Origin, why are You crying, O Beloved piece of Land?" I asked.

The Land replied, *"I have not been treated with such tenderness (that you have shown to Me) in decades! No one has ever stopped to pick Me up and notice Me for what I am. All that people have done is dug into My heart, trampled all over Me and erected structures over Me as they pleased.*

There was a time when they dug Me up with little hoes and shovels. Later, they dug Me up with machines, tractors and excavators. They poured concrete all over Me and paved Me with asphalt. They plunged Me into darkness until I could no longer be seen!

"Amyn, you saw what I was as I thrived under the Ocean. I was home to the creatures that treated Me with such respect. Look at Me now! When the Origin created the Earth, the Land was laid down with all its beauties — mountains, forests, rivers, Oceans and all the surfaces that you know — with a deep hand of tenderness. It was almost like how a mother lays down the blankets gently on the crib of her baby, so as to ensure that the baby is comfortable at all times. This is how I was laid down by the Origin.

"I was filled with Love, for I was to become the home to all Creation. As a humble Servant to the Origin, I offered all that I could to every living creature that came and drew from Me its needs. When I give, I find nothing but joy, for I am an aspect of Divine Generosity. The Origin is the Giver of all things. As time went by, all I did was to give of Myself, again and again. I gave to all Creation for this is why I was Created. I was never to belong to anyone but the Origin.

"Then, Amyn, people came along with all their ways and desires. They drew boundaries all over Me and decided who could and could not set foot

on Me. I now had a so-called "master," the greedy human being. Suddenly, I belonged to one owner, who claimed to be the "Proprietor" of Me. He even put up his name on Me to tell all the rest of his companions that he "owned" Me. I was sold like a slave, over and over again. They gave Me the name of "Real Estate." My identity was no longer of any importance. A value was placed upon Me which depended upon how many tall buildings were erected on and around Me. Today, I am a "Lot for Sale." How great was I at one time as I existed in pride, dignity and honour under the Ocean. Now, I am a "Lot for Sale." Look at how everyone tramples all over Me. They drive their vehicles on Me. They dump their garbage on Me. I have nothing left in Me to give, Amyn. I am drained and barren. I cannot even give birth to a blade of grass anymore, My dear Amyn. Look at what people have made Me! Do you call this justice, Amyn? By the command of the Origin, all I have done is to give, and all people have done is to take. I was never created as a slave to be used and sold over and over again. This could not have been what the Origin had in mind! Then, O Beloved Amyn, explain to Me why this has happened to Me. Crimes have been committed over Me. People have been killed over Me. So much evil has been manifested over Me. O dear, dear Amyn, tell Me why, for I can never understand what has happened to Me!"

I brought the dirt to my lips and kissed it gently. The tears that rolled from my eyes fell on the beloved dirt. I held my palm open and said, "O Beloved Land, I am truly sorry for what has happened to You. Indeed, You were given form as a supreme generosity from the Origin. You were made home to so many. No being can ever 'own' You for You belong to the Origin, and thus, You belong to *all* Creation. The claims that people have placed on You are false, for You know only too well that when people die, they are buried within You. From You, they are dispersed into Infinity. I am sorry that You have been treated this way. My heart cries out for You for being plunged into darkness with such turmoil. You are indeed barren today for You cannot give birth to even a single blade of grass. But, O Beloved Land, You are still You. People will come and people will go. But You will always be You.

"Therefore, be patient, O Beloved Land, for a time will come when You will be freed again. You never were a captive or slave of any human being, and You never will be. I know that in a short while, a tall building will be built on You to house thousands of human beings. They will take You for granted because they will simply think of You as being plain pavement. However, do not look at Yourself as the captive. You do have power over what happens on You. If you trembled only slightly, all the tall buildings that have been built on You would come crashing down. That is how weak and temporary human structures are! A short time ago, You trembled a little and look what happened to Los Angeles! Where were the powerful human beings that claimed to own

You? They were running for their lives. All I can say to You, O Beloved Land, is have faith in Your Origin. You are fulfilling Your purpose and although You are put through such pain, You are truly fulfilling Your purpose. Civilizations will come and go, as they build and destroy themselves. You will always continue to be, and *that* is important."

I kissed the Land once again and felt very sad as I heard its sobs of pain. I said to the Land, "The end of this chapter is very close. With all the things that humans have done to You here, and particularly with all the evil that has occurred here, humanity has lost the privilege of living on You. Soon, My dear, very soon, there will come a day when You will shake violently and through this shaking You will cleanse Yourself of all the abuse that has occurred on You. The time will be 4:00 a.m. when this happens. This will be the time of Your liberation. I will not give the date when Your liberation is to occur for I do not wish to instill fear in anyone. But, My dear One, it will be soon, very soon. After You have shaken off the evil over You, the Ocean will come crashing all over You to cleanse You completely and to restore upon You the dignity that You enjoyed once upon a time, when You were home to the creatures of the Ocean. Your ordeal will then be over. Darkness will be over. You will once again belong to *all* the Creation of the Origin.

"O Beloved Land, promise Me that when You are liberated, You will tenderly receive all the human beings that are buried within You at the time of Your liberation.

For them too it will be a moment of liberation, for they will be relieved from the evils and pains of this world. You cannot and will not judge them for their deeds. The only One who can judge them is the Origin, who is the Creator of all. I bid You farewell, O Beloved Land. I know Your liberation is close. I congratulate You for all Your endurance and admire Your spirit. You will no longer be barren. You will give birth again to so many life forms. A Mother is always a Mother. Just when You feel that there is no way out, suddenly, You will be completely free. That is the justice of the Origin. Generosity is You and Generosity will always be You. You can never be barren for she that gives can never *ever* be barren. That is the Law of Giving.

Received on May 26, 1995.

THIRTY

THE *B*LACK *R*OSE

I opened the gates to the Rose Garden and quietly but gently entered what one may describe as Heaven on Earth. In this garden were roses of all colours. I was greeted by the sweetest fragrances of the most beautiful roses. I turned to my right and saw an unending bed of yellow roses. To my left was a similar bed of red roses. The Sun was just rising and the dewdrops gently reflected the Sunlight that greeted the roses and their buds. In the bed of yellow roses grew tall, healthy stalks with rich green foliage, surrounded by buds and fully blossomed flowers. Of course, the thorns always took their appropriate place. Likewise, the bed of red roses was also a healthy array of colours, mainly green and red.

I looked ahead of me and in the distance I saw a ball of Light that quietly stood in the middle of the path that I was treading on. As I walked towards this Light, it remained completely still. I walked on for awhile and although it seemed like I was getting closer to the Light, I was not making the kind of progress one would expect as one walked straight towards a still object! I looked to my right and was now flanked by a bed of pink roses. The leaves and the stems of these roses looked weak and undernourished. The petals of these roses had fallen to the ground to form a pink carpet. Compared to the rich beds of red and yellow roses, this bed appeared to be poor and weak. It lacked the lustre and Life that I had just seen. The fragrance was weak too. Then I looked to my left and saw a bed of white roses. This bed looked poorer than the pink bed. The leaves and stems of these white rose bushes were turning brown. All the petals had fallen off from the roses. The buds that had not blossomed drooped weakly on their stems, suggesting that their ultimate fate was to dry off and fall to the ground without the white petals having their chance to taste the rich atmosphere of Life. There was almost no fragrance in the air by this point.

Then, as I looked ahead of me, I saw the ball of Light. It was no ordinary ball. It was about as tall as me, and I am six feet tall! The Light had an even brightness all round. However, around its circumference I could see haloes of Light with lower intensities. As I took three steps forward, something miraculous happened! I saw a rosebud emerge right in the centre of the Light! It must have been at least six inches long. Then this rosebud began to open and behold, in the centre of this beautiful Light was a Black Rose! I have never seen a Black Rose before. Surrounded by this beautiful Light, the Rose gave off a radiance of its own, despite the fact that the colour black is not known to radiate Light in our material world.

I continued to walk towards the Light, and now I began to close in rapidly. I stopped as I got to within three feet. I could now smell a beautiful fragrance. But it was not that of roses! It was a familiar scent. Where had I encountered this scent before?

It was sandalwood! And behold, it was the same fragrance that I had experienced when I met the Messenger in the mist (in Chapter 14, *The New Land*), the Messenger whose face I could not see, except for the glow in His eyes. My heart leapt with joy. I cried out to the Light, "Is it You, O Beloved Messenger of the Origin that has taught me so much? Is it You, the Beloved Soul that taught me of my Mission on that beautiful misty morning?"

From the Light came the familiar Voice that said, *"Yes, indeed, Amyn, it is Me, but as you can see, I have a different form. In front of you, I am a ball of Light. In the centre of Me is the Black Rose, a flower that you have never seen, because it is not of your world. My dear Amyn, I have come to teach you about another dimension of Life in the world that you presently live in. This is a dimension that has its roots in the Unseen."*

I replied with excitement, "I am so happy to be with You again. When I see You, I see a mirror in whose image I see me. Indeed, O Beloved One, You and I are One, aren't we?"

The Messenger replied, *"Yes indeed, Amyn, We are One. You are a physical manifestation of Me in the world of material dimensions. Your Essence is indeed Me, and Our Essence is the Origin. I have come to you in this garden of roses to show you an aspect of living that you must teach to humanity. Amyn, in one single rose garden, you saw so much. You walked through the gates (which I led you to) to be greeted by two rich, luscious beds of roses, the yellow one to your right and the red one to your left. The fragrance from these beds was heavenly. You could see that these two beds thrived in the soil, and gave such a pleasant and rich identity to the garden as you walked through. My Beloved Amyn, what was the difference between the yellow bed to your right and the red bed to your left?"*

I thought for a moment and replied, "O Beloved One, both the beds had the same leaves, thorns, stems and soil. The only difference was the colour of the roses."

The Messenger then said, *"That is correct, Amyn. The only difference between the two beds was that of colour. Otherwise, everything else was identical. The roses were indeed just roses. Then, Amyn, did you wonder why the yellow ones all grouped together to the right and the red ones to the left?"*

I quietly replied, "I suppose the Gardener wanted it that way."

The Messenger replied, *"Yes and no, Amyn. The Gardener did indeed plant the roses that way. He then nourished them and gave them health. But once they had been planted they also did have a will of their own by which they could grow and spread. These are roses that had been given the power to spread and integrate. But they chose not to. Instead, the yellow bed proudly stood on its own as did the red bed! All that separated them was colour. The stronger they grew, the more superior they felt over all other roses. But, Amyn, all they are is roses. You can pluck them at your will and they can do nothing!*

By this time, I had begun to think more deeply about what was going on. The Messenger then said, *"Are you now wondering about the pink and white beds that are falling apart and dying?"*

I quickly replied, "Yes, O Beloved One, that is exactly what I am wondering about."

The Messenger then said, *"The pink bed was strong and luscious, as was the white bed. They too stood strong on their own. Then, the Gardener planted the yellow and red beds. As these new beds grew, the pink and white beds allowed nutrients from their soil to go over and feed the two young beds. The pink and white beds took the first step in sharing and spreading. You see, at one time, the pink bed was red, but it integrated with the white to become pink. After all, roses are roses. The joy and success of the pink and white beds was such that they wanted to share it with the new yellow and red beds. Remember that the pink and white beds lived in the garden well before the yellow and the red beds came along. They learned to love and share for they were in touch with Nature. But as they began to give of themselves to the yellow and red beds, they began to shrivel and die, because these new beds just took and gave back nothing in return. My dear Amyn, the only difference between red, yellow, pink and white is colour. Roses are roses. You can pluck them at any time you please. But, now the original inhabitants of the Garden that had gained Knowledge and wisdom are dying because the new beds (red and yellow) are taking away everything from them and giving back nothing in return. These new beds may look strong and healthy and have a strong fragrance, but they are indeed hollow and have no wisdom or Knowledge compared to their predecessor neighbours, the pink and the white roses."*

Now it all began to make sense to me. The Messenger then said, *"Amyn, look at the history of your world. Look at the Native Indians of America, the Eskimos, Incas and all other such races. Do they not remind you of the pink and white roses? And look around you at the strong, developed nations. Then think about the red and yellow roses. The only difference between them all is colour and perceived strength. Do you now see around you, in your material world, the story of the Rose Garden, Amyn?"*

I replied, "Yes, indeed, O Beloved One, I see the story of the Rose Garden all around me. And throughout the history of humanity, I can see Rose Garden after Rose Garden."

The Messenger then asked, *"My dear Amyn, what else do you see here?"*

I immediately replied, "The Black Rose, O Beloved One. This is the Rose that stands in the centre of Your Light. It is so beautiful and radiant. But the fragrance is one of sandalwood and not roses."

The Messenger then replied, *"Amyn, the Black Rose is a Sign from the Origin to Humanity. It is a Rose of power and radiance, despite the fact that the colour black does not radiate Light. In this alone is another Sign to Humanity. Whilst you are in the Rose Garden, you see roses of different colours in the states of their own fate. But, this Black Rose is not just a rose. You cannot just pluck it like you can the others. I want you to tell the world about the Black Rose. It is a Sign from the Origin; a Sign of Mercy, and yet, a Sign of Warning. Take a close look at Life in the world, its values and its ways. Take a close look at what all the Messengers have said to the people. Then look at the pink and white rose beds. Then look at the red and yellow rose beds. Remember that each bed lay either to your right or to your left. But the Black Rose stands right in front of you, in the centre of Light. These are clues for the wise ones to recognize the meaning of the Black Rose."*

I knew that the Beloved Messenger had given to me the Signs of the Origin to be passed on to the human race. There is a Sign of Mercy and a Sign of Warning. The Light in front of me began to fade and behold, in front of me lay a beautiful bed of roses! However, they were not ordinary roses. *They were Black Roses....*

Received on May 29, 1995.

THIRTY-ONE

THE $\mathcal{P}$APYRUS $\mathcal{R}$EED

I hear the Divine Voice say to me, *"Talk about the papyrus reed, Amyn. Talk about what the Angels saw. Share with humanity a perspective of the growth of Knowledge in all aspects of Life in the world. Where is humanity headed? Share the story of the Angels, so that those that may read this Message may learn, by the Mercy of the Origin."*

On a bright, sunny morning in Egypt, women crowded along the banks of the River Nile to collect drinking water, wash their clothes and bathe themselves and their children. Little Malik, who was about twelve years old, walked away from the group of women as they did their chores. He walked further down the banks of the Nile, where the vegetation grew denser. Soon he was in the midst of papyrus reeds that were taller than him! As Malik slowly walked through the reeds, he was being

201

watched by two Angels, Luminus and Cyrus. They looked at Malik intently as he pulled out his sharp little knife and proceeded to cut several papyrus reeds. He carried these reeds back to where the women were working along the bank of the river. He laid down the reeds and proceeded to spread them open.

Luminus looked at Cyrus and said, "Here starts the next chapter of learning for humanity! Do you remember the time when the family that lived in the caves during the Stone Age started to draw pictures on the walls of the caves? Do you remember the child trying to explain to his parents what he had seen, but no one could understand him? In desperation, he picked up the rock and tried to draw a picture on the cave wall so that his family could understand what he had seen."

Cyrus, who was deep in thought, said, "Yes, therein started the form of written communication. People from those times left Knowledge on cave walls and stone tablets. The reader had to travel to the Knowledge. That was the norm!"

Luminus then said, "Humanity thought that it had come a long ways through the achievement of inscribing Knowledge from the mind to the stone walls and tablets. How proud everyone was about this!"

Cyrus then said, "When I was with the other Angels in the Garden, I was told that rather than people travelling to Knowledge, it will be possible for Knowledge to travel to people. Behold, look what Malik is doing! He is producing a medium that is a lot easier to transport than the stone tablets. He is discovering that he can write on the papyrus! This act of a twelve-year-old will now change the course of history of this world!"

Luminus was most excited. He exclaimed, "This will lead to a great development of the human mind. They will write down their thoughts and others will read these thoughts freely. This will become the medium for the teaching and spreading of Knowledge. This will dominate communication throughout the world. One simple discovery by a child, and everything is about to change!"

Cyrus then said, "The Origin did not permit the discovery of papyrus through Malik until now, because the mind of the human being was not ready to receive this medium as a means to transfer Knowledge. The stars, who are the Aspects of Knowledge, are now ready for this process to occur. Remember, the stars have a great role to play in the evolution of Knowledge in humanity."

From this day on came a major evolution in the world. Humanity concentrated on perfecting the art of making and distributing paper. It all started from one single event. Centuries later, Cyrus and Luminus, whose job it was to monitor Knowledge and learning, continued to watch the developments in communications throughout the world. Ordinary people could write letters and send them to people far away. Access to paper created money and currency. The cowry shell was gone! People wrote agreements with one another. What was laid on paper began to rule the mind. Then came newsprint and this led humanity rapidly down a path of simultaneous growth and deterioration. The growth came from sharing of information. The deterioration came from spreading negative ideologies and values through newsprint.

Luminus said to Cyrus, "It has taken hundreds of years for humanity to evolve from the time of Malik's discovery to this level. But now, each year that goes by, humanity is evolving at a pace that is ten times faster than before! The awareness of humanity has grown. There is a great need, which did not exist before, for rapid transfer of information. This need will drive new inventions."

Cyrus then said, "I heard in the Garden that humanity is now ready to make further strides that will change the world again, even faster. They will send voice across the world in waves and pictures. The time has come for this."

Luminus then said, "There goes another round of change in this world. Distances will shrink and people will transmit more Knowledge even more freely. You see, Cyrus, the quantity of Knowledge in the Universe is infinite. Humanity has learned to draw on minute fragments of this Knowledge. And tiny doses of this Knowledge cause major changes in the world each time! Can you imagine what large doses of this Knowledge could do to the world?"

Cyrus, who was still in deep thought, said, "The rate at which humanity will draw on the Knowledge from the Universe is very carefully regulated, as you know.

Humanity could destroy itself instantaneously if this control were not there."

Luminus then said, "The cavemen sparked off a small change, and Malik sparked off a bigger one. What makes me sad is to see that humanity is losing its happiness as more and more of these changes come about. People are drifting away from one another. All that matters is the material."

Cyrus replied, "In the Gardens of the Angels, it is said that the humans will transmit information from little balls in outer space which will be called satellites. Luminus smiled and said, "This takes humanity through another round of change! They have also developed these little things called computers, which have given them the power to multiply their Knowledge storage and transfer ability. This little gadget is now almost in every home and workplace."

Cyrus, the deep thinker, said, "One more scrap of Knowledge and the world now doesn't resemble Malik's times! He would be shocked to see what he sparked off!"

Luminus then predicted, "In the Gardens of the Angels, it is said that the next thing that humanity will be able to do is to transmit Knowledge through thought itself! With each step of evolution, the quantity of Knowledge stored and transferred is growing."

The wise Cyrus pointed out, "I saw a scientist who was trying to train a mouse to walk through a hundred-step maze. The poor creature was confused after getting past the second bend in the maze. It seemed completely bewildered and yet there were ninety-eight bends ahead for it to cross. At the second bend, the mouse seemed to have lost touch with what it was before it entered the maze! I am apprehensive about what will happen to humanity as it goes past the first bend in the maze of Universal Knowledge!"

Luminus then said, "Each minor curve within the first bend of this maze has changed the world completely! Humanity has lost touch with its true self. Each little scrap of Knowledge creates an even greater illusion in their little world, which completely engrosses them."

The wise Cyrus then declared, "If humans knew the secret behind the Knowledge of the Universe, they would be totally amazed about how simple everything is!"

Luminus replied, "Of course, the entire Knowledge of the Universe rests within the human being. But their illusions take them very far away from the Truth!"

Cyrus, with his hand on his chin, replied, "People remind me of the fish that swim in the Ocean of water, but keep jumping out to catch little raindrops."

Luminus chuckled and said, "Cyrus, speak softly. They might hear you!"

"Well, Luminus, from the time of the cavemen to Malik to today they have caught six raindrops in all!"

My dear friends, contemplate on what Cyrus has said about the fish that swim in the Ocean of water who keep jumping out to catch little raindrops! There is a lot of wisdom in His words. Perhaps it is time to stop jumping out of the water and to start diving deeper into the water! Something to think about....

Received on June 19, 1995.

$\mathcal{M}$ESSAGE TO THE $\mathcal{S}$CIENTIST

My dear friends, the following seven Chapters contain very special Revelations on Science. To best understand the depth of what is being Revealed, it is essential that they be read together in *numerical order*. Important concepts are Revealed, stage by stage, which grow further in depth from Chapter to Chapter. These concepts are advanced in nature and will represent Science as the world will come to know it a hundred years from now! Actually, it is my sincere hope that this process will occur much sooner!

May you be blessed with the ability to understand and learn from these very special Revelations.

Part 1 — Information Flow: Evolution,
          Genetics and Energy

Part 2 — Limitations Of Scientific Laws

Part 3 — Discovery Of New Senses:
          Telepathy and Powers To Heal

$\mathscr{M}$ESSAGE TO THE $\mathscr{S}$CIENTIST – $\mathscr{P}$ART 1

INFORMATION FLOW:
EVOLUTION, GENETICS AND ENERGY

I hear the Divine Voice say, *"Amyn, you have been blessed with a strong background in Science, for the simple reason that you must accelerate awareness in humanity of the seriously conflicting changes that are being experienced between human beings and their environment. You must share Our Message on this subject for the sake of humanity and all the creatures on planet Earth. The scientists of today do not understand the greater consequences of their actions, particularly when they are dealing with forms of energy such as nuclear energy, or fields of Science such as genetic engineering. Therefore, although you are no* authority on these subjects, you must make every effort to warn humanity of the irreversible damage that is occurring on the beautiful planet Earth.

"We have created man and woman to live on this Earth and to accomplish the Mission(s) that We have set forth for each human being. The Earth is made up of land, water and air. Just as the human being is Our creation of the land, We have created dolphins in the Ocean, to be the human's aquatic counterpart. We have bestowed intellect in both humans and dolphins. They are of common ancestry.

"Humans have evolved rapidly within their surroundings and this evolution has caused them to change their surroundings. Look at the plain green fields that today have become concrete forests. Therefore, whilst evolution occurs to adapt Our creation to its surroundings, humans have caused a change within this cycle of evolution itself. For the longest time, Nature catalyzed evolution. But humans, by application of their intellect, rightly or wrongly, caused complex changes within their own surroundings. This has triggered a response by Nature that has begun to cause further changes in humans to adapt to the new surroundings and way of life that they have created. Cancer, which is the mutation of cells, in essence is a direct result of this complex interaction and interference that humans have imposed within the process of evolution. According to Nature's way, the human body needs to change rapidly to keep up with its changing surroundings and way of life. Humans continue to accelerate this change to their own serious detriment.

"Nature's Laws of Evolution are based upon transmission of 'Information' from the surroundings (environment) to the genes of humans and vice versa. There are also sub-genes which exist within the genetic framework that are part of the 'Informational Flow'. These sub-genes have not as yet been discovered because they are micro-Pulses that leave no trace of their existence. Smaller than the sub-genes is another class of low-level Flow channels for 'Information'. Below this there are more lower levels (classes) of 'Information Flow' that interact with their respective upper levels. This interaction is very much like the interaction between different 'decks' of Energy. Students of genetics must endeavour to learn to identify the sub-genetic levels that underlie genes in all living creatures. (Amyn, you have never studied genetics and what you are writing is from Inspiration from the Source of the Creation.)

"In other parts of the Universe there are numerous intelligent life forms that are intellectually equal to or more advanced than dolphins and humans. The application of their intelligence is always conducted with utmost sensitivity to the overall balance that must prevail within the Universe. There have been life forms, like our

Creation on Mars, that annihilated themselves through incompatible changes that they triggered within themselves and their surroundings. This is exactly where the human race is currently headed! The absence of growth of plant life in the deserts is a rather simple illustration of such conflicts with the surroundings. In some cases, humans have created deserts by cutting down forests. The creation of deserts was an early warning sign. Cancer was the next sign because conflicting 'Information Flow' between the genes of humans and their surroundings have caused uncontrollable mutations. The AIDS virus was the next product of this change. It will claim many lives. The current matrix of 'Information Flow' is such that viruses such as AIDS will further mutate within themselves to create new and more deadly strains. The immune system was the target of AIDS. The nervous system is the target of the next strain to come. And there will be more! Unless significant corrective changes are made, humanity will force its evolution in the direction of its rapid obliteration!

"If the rapid spread of deadly diseases such as cancer, AIDS and the more deadly ones yet to come is to be controlled, humanity is going to have to learn much from its counterpart in the Ocean, the dolphin.

"Look at the way the dolphin lives and interacts with its environment and its fellow creatures in the Ocean. Whilst it is a fact that dolphins have a

greater intellectual capacity than humans, dolphins have also learned to recognize and manage the forces of evolution that surround them. They do not change their environment dramatically, as humans have done. They live within a genetic energy and 'Informational Balance' that keeps their bodies and activities in total harmony with their surroundings. Indeed, change is occurring within the dolphins, but it is very much in the correct direction of 'Information Flow'. Humans, on the contrary, have created massive conflicts between the 'Information' and its direction of flow. The net result is the start of chaos as you are currently experiencing in the world. The worst part is whilst the more intelligent dolphin has done nothing to hurt humans and their environment, the converse is not true. Humans are in fact heavily endangering the aquatic environment through careless and needless pollution. This will, in time, trigger too rapid a change in the aquatic environment which will negatively influence the 'Information Flow'. This will cause cancers and epidemics in dolphins, whales and all the other aquatic creatures.

"It is said that what takes decades to create can be destroyed in seconds. In a relative time scale, it has taken billions of years for the cycle of evolution to bring the Earth to the level it is at today. Yet the uncontrolled and complex interacting changes that humans have triggered within their environment could indeed destroy a majority of the life forms that exist today on Earth.

"Humanity's indulgence in genetic engineering, which is a field that they know very little about, will unleash a change that is well beyond their control. They are playing with powers that can cause irreparable damage to the Earth and all its life forms. Genetic engineering is a field that is far more deadly than nuclear energy. The experience of Russia and Chernobyl is a good example of the devastation that can be caused by mismanagement of nuclear power. Look at the genetic composition of the generations that have suffered from this contamination. Explain to the scientists who consider themselves wise that they must stop playing with forces that they do not understand. Do they really know why the radioactivity in Chernobyl has caused mutants in the current and coming child population? Give them this hint. They do not know that sub-genes exist as Pulses that carry and react to 'Information'. These Pulses leave no trace of themselves but do leave a reaction or imprint within the Genetic Code. The radioactive energy directly influences these sub-genetic Pulses, because the energy of the Pulses, that is in the less than microvolt level, is heavily overshadowed by fields that the radioactivity causes around them. This causes mutations.

"Humanity's choice of energy sources is extremely poor. A lot of pollution and interference in 'Information Flow' comes from the use of oil and its derivatives, electrical and nuclear energy. For those naive ones that believe in the effectiveness *of radioactive shields, tell them that there is no such thing.* Just because their instruments cannot monitor low levels of energy does not mean that a radioactive shield truly exists. *We told you of sub-genes and the 'deck', all of which are based upon energies that are currently immeasurable. The radioactivity that leaves the so-called shield has devastating effects on the sub-genes and the 'Order' of 'Information Assembly'.* Never assume that because you cannot measure something, it does not exist.

"Extensive efforts must be directed to alternative sources of energy. It is not necessary to work in megavolts, for such high energy levels are unnatural phenomena. Nature works at the micro level. Of course if the means of energy generation, transmission and conversion are highly inefficient, one is forced to operate at the mega level. The greatest single energy reservoir on Earth is water. *Water was the by-product of the conversion of energy to matter at the time of the Earth's formation. Resources must be directed to tap into the energy reserves of water. This research must look at the water molecule and at the submolecular level. It is like a diamond with cleavages. If you try to crack the water molecule, you are trying to cut through a diamond at its hardest point. This is why energy has not been drawn from water to date. Look for the cleavages, where a small amount of energy can trigger a large release of energy from*

water. You can have engines that use salt water as the fuel and discharge fresh water as emissions.

"Remember that the planet Earth has a finite amount of water in different forms. Hence, by using energy from water, a process can be developed that is in harmony with this finite water quantity within the planet, because the only variable is the actual form of the water. Of course, this will change the economic framework of the world drastically, but it is about high time that this occurred anyway! There would be a complete re-distribution of wealth since energy will be abundant and accessible. Pollution will drop sharply. There will be no power transmission lines. Each home will be powered by a water cell. The quality of life of people will improve dramatically. The conflict with the 'Information Flow' will be reduced. Even humanity's natural and ethical values will change since supply/ demand of energy will no longer be a factor. The very poor may not remain poor. People will gain back their sense of identity with respect to their Inner Selves. This will be a change in the right direction. Just like the invention of paper caused a major change in the world, this form of water-powered engine will dramatically alter the course of human history. The energy sources used today account for a major proportion of the world's pollution. This can be eliminated through one single invention. Remember, the micro-level energy is the way to go in seeking and exploiting the cleavages in the submolecular structure of water.

"Once again, look at the dolphin. Learn from it. We are not saying that Science must not advance, for that is a process that must occur. But dolphins mastered the advancement of Science well before humans by understanding the interactive forces within themselves and their environment. There are some very simple but meaningful answers in their ways.

"Amyn, this is a Chapter that must be taken most seriously. The Origin, who Created the Earth and all its life forms, knows best how the puzzle fits. A warning from the level of the Origin must be heeded with great seriousness. The future of the human race is in its own hands. It can change, or it can destroy itself and the rest of Earth's life forms. If the dolphin polluted the world in a manner that endangered humans, it is rather obvious that humanity would wage war on the dolphin. Yet today the converse is true and the dolphin has done nothing about it yet. Learn from this. It could not be spelt out to you more clearly. Warnings such as these must be viewed as blessings rather than as a challenge."

Received on June 21, 1995.

My dear friends, as I wrote this Chapter, I caught glimpses of Knowledge that are very deep and that we are a long ways away from appreciating. I will do all I can to enhance this awareness throughout the world. Help me in my task, for it truly is the task for our future. We must leave the right legacy for our future generations. May we succeed in heeding the warnings that we have just received....

$\mathscr{M}$ESSAGE TO THE $\mathscr{S}$CIENTIST – $\mathscr{P}$ART 2

LIMITATIONS OF SCIENTIFIC LAWS

"Think further about the discovery of Our Creation. We Create and allow Science to discover. The scientist is merely an explorer who finds elements and aspects of the Creation. The scientist is not the Creator, but merely an explorer. The correct frame of mind for a scientist seeking to discover is one of humility. There is no room for pride or vanity for that will only close the doors of the School that the scientist is so dearly attempting to enter. This is the School of the Knowledge of the Universe. Ask yourselves, what is Knowledge? It is not something you can see, and yet Knowledge is based upon the principle of receiving, assimilating and applying 'Information'. When We talked about the 'Information Flow' in the context of genetics and

evolution, We provided Enlightenment to the reader of the Message on one of the important aspects of Knowledge as it relates to 'Information'. Knowledge emanates from the very lowest energy levels in Creation all the way to the very highest levels.

"You must think deeply about Knowledge. When the human mind receives Knowledge, an imprint is made by the 'Information Pulses' within the brain, which is in many ways similar to the imprints made by the Pulses in sub-genes on the Genetic Code. These imprints are aspects of the reception and assimilation of 'Information'. The application of this 'Information' often manifests itself in a physical change or changes that are visible to the eye. Take cancer, for example. The conflict of 'Information' yields a format of 'Information' that is imprinted within the Genetic Code by the Pulses within the sub-genes. The 'Information' is assimilated within the Genetic Code, which then applies this 'Information' to yield cell mutation. Hence you see cancer. Therefore, remember that it is a three-step process, of transfer, assimilation and application.

"Look at forms of energy. What is energy? Why does it have forms? The rules are similar. Energy in itself is 'Information-based' and hence it has the ability to flow. This is why energy transfer is an accepted practice. The assimilation of energy occurs at two ends, i.e., at the source and at the true point of application. There must be a harmonic balance between the source and point of application. Look at electrical energy. When it is *generated, an assimilation of this energy occurs, which is then transported down the transfer system to the light bulb. At the bulb, this energy once again assimilates on the basis of its fundamental 'Information-flow' principles. The application yields light and heat, one of which is visible and the other which can be felt.*

"Now look at nuclear energy. This is the energy of fission. Atoms release energy through fission. The instability of these atoms is caused by an 'Information input'. Assimilation occurs within the atom. The application is manifested through energy released by the splitting or fission process. This energy is convertible to heat or electricity and then transmitted onwards. You see, the three-step cycle of 'Information flow' governs all energy generation, transfer and application processes. Think of the energy level of the Information that triggered the fission. It is a very low-level energy compared to the output of fission. This is a principle of propulsion that humanity has not learned as yet *because they are limited by the so called 'Law' that states, 'Action and Reaction are Equal and Opposite'. The propulsion methods for rockets, aircraft and automobiles, for example, are based on this incorrect presupposition, which really must* never *be referred to as a Law.*

In Science, there are no *Laws. If an explorer follows Laws, his or her discovery will be limited to the boundaries of what the Laws dictate.*

"Our Creation travels throughout space and the Universe with such speed that humans are unable to comprehend. Yes, there is life in other parts of the Universe. Yes, Our Creation does travel using very natural methods of propulsion. Humans have limited themselves to the level of energy application in accordance with the Law of Action and Reaction being Equal and Opposite. Now go down one level below macro energy to the 'Information Flow' level. At this level, a small action can yield a massive reaction. Therein lies the secret to true propulsion.

"Do you want a great parallel to this explanation, Amyn? Of course you do! Look at 'Thought' itself. How fast can Thought travel? What is the basis of Thought? 'Information Flow' is the answer. And a small trigger of 'Information' in the mind yields a great instantaneous distance of travel in Thought! If the so-called Law of Action and Reaction were truly applicable to Thought, most humans would suffer from overheated or charred brains!

"You must share this Knowledge with scientists who, if they have an open mind, may start to search for discoveries at a new level, which is the level of 'Information'. They must get away from the Energy level because when a tall tower is to be built, one must start at the foundation and not at its uppermost tip. At the level of the foundation, there is considerable room for growth and movement. Hence, there is 'Flexibility'. At the tip of the tower at its highest point, one's ability to move is severely *limited. This limitation brings about the creation and adherence to Laws that truly are not always correct.*

"Now, once Science goes down to the 'Information' level, humans will be able to recognize and measure what forms of energy are beneficial and what forms are devastating in relation to their surroundings. Nuclear energy will be dropped immediately once this realization occurs. Therefore, remember, tell them to have an open mind. Tell them to not restrict themselves by Laws of Science. Tell them to move from the uppermost tip of the tower, which is the macro level, to the foundation level which is the micro 'Information' level. They will be a lot more free to move there. There will be no restrictions. Then they will make real and rapid discoveries. A time will come when humanity will mend its position with respect to its surroundings. Like our other Creations in the Universe, human beings will be able to travel the greatest of distances in the shortest of time. Energy and its use or abuse will take a new dimension based upon a real understanding and ability to measure 'Information', whose three simple principles of transfer, assimilation and application will yield the simplest of answers to propulsion and many other aspects of Science.

"The ones of lower understanding will ridicule what you have written. Others will stop to think about it. The leaders amongst them will take steps

to direct their investigations according to the hints that We have given to them here. Remember, all you are is a Messenger. All that We expect of you is to correctly convey this Message. How it is received and interpreted is not within your power or responsibility. Through this Chapter, a completely new page in Science can be turned. And there are no Laws to comply with. No one has the authority to make Laws. When you go down to the 'Information' level, you will realize that Flexibility *is the norm and Laws of Science as you know them are in* conflict *with this* Flexibility. *Can you start to see why human beings have created a conflict within themselves, their surroundings and the process of evolution? Abandon all Laws of Science and search with openness. That is the true attribute of Science — 'openness and humility in the search for the Creation'."*

Received on June 22, 1995.

THIRTY-FOUR

$\mathscr{M}$ESSAGE TO THE $\mathscr{S}$CIENTIST $-$ $\mathscr{P}$ART 3
DISCOVERY OF NEW SENSES:
TELEPATHY AND POWERS TO HEAL

"Write about the senses that make up
Consciousness. In the material world, each being
is confined to a limited number of senses which
include sight, hearing, smell, taste and touch. The
combination of these senses gives one awareness
of one's surroundings. Each of these senses is
governed by the level and flow of 'Information'.
Each sense receives this 'Information', assimilates
it and then applies it to yield the sensation that has
been triggered by the 'Information'. Therefore, there
are five known faculties of senses in a human
being. Recognizing the 'Information' level will open
up additional senses.

"Look at dolphins. They have a sense of telepathy. They emit 'Information' from within their brains, which is picked up by the recipients. Human beings too can exercise this sense of telepathy. This has not been feasible because of humanity's confused interaction with its surroundings and the constant conflict between 'Information Flows' around human beings. The sense of telepathy is an exercise of Thought transmission through very low energy levels within the prescribed pattern of 'Information Flow'.

"Then there is the sense of Self Protection and Healing. The human body does not need large doses of medication to protect itself from diseases or to help it heal from ailments. The protective mechanisms in humans, i.e., the white blood cells and related organisms, operate on the basis of 'Information Flow'. The cells receive 'Information' pertaining to an intrusion and they configure themselves to eliminate the intruder. The human mind can also convey 'Information' to these cells to go into combat or to heal a particular area. This sense has been totally numbed in humanity by the high chemical intake within the body and conflicts with the environment. The human body is a complex Network of 'Information Assembly' and 'Flow'. One can heal oneself by pure communication internally at low energy levels. Throughout history, herbalists have cured people by natural means. In reality, these herbs carried 'Information Codes' that triggered instructions for healing. In the same way,

through the transfer of 'Information', humans can heal one another.

"The powers to heal are not magical, rather, they stem from a deep internal awareness of how the 'Information Network' functions. Those that are aware of their Inner Selves and who have a greater level of esoteric awareness can quickly recognize and apply these methods of healing. Jesus Christ (Peace be upon Him) was highly aware of the esoteric plane. From this came His powers to heal, for indeed He had been granted awareness of the 'Information Assembly' and 'Network' from the Origin, who is the Source of all Creation. People mistook His powers for sorcery or magic. However, in reality, He had been granted the ability to transmit and manage 'Information' at the low energy levels.

"Meditation and a deep inner search will awaken one to the powers and realities that exist within oneself. With five senses, the human being is truly nowhere near as aware as he or she can be. People who are short of hearing or eyesight or any other sense are looked upon as disabled. They are treated as if they are incomplete! Well, all those with only five senses are disabled by their very own definition, for there are a great many senses that are not being utilized within the human being. Before taking physical form, each Soul possessed ninety-nine senses. The encagement in the body reduced this to five. Yet, opening up to the reality of 'Information Flow' and the 'Networks' that govern *the Self can increase the number of senses significantly. Tell people to ponder over this for there are wonders that await them within themselves. Science is ready to start to drop down to the 'Information' level. When this occurs, the changes will be rapid. When humans can increase their senses and awareness, they will become more content, for a deeper understanding of the realities of Creation will come about within them. For this you must all pray...."*

Received on June 23, 1995.

$\mathscr{M}$ESSAGE TO THE $\mathscr{S}$CIENTIST – $\mathscr{P}$ART 4

THE ATOM

"What is an atom? What does it represent? What are the components of an atom? You may say that they include electrons, neutrons and protons with their appropriate electrical charges. Then, you may say that every substance is indeed a composite of millions of atoms. Are you correct? Perhaps in a small way, you are correct. But, is the atom indeed the lowest common denominator in everything? There are levels that go much lower down than the atom itself. You may call them fields or force fields comprising energy that has taken itself to the 'Information' level.

"Anything you examine does indeed boil itself down to the level of 'Information'. For example, look at the electron and the proton. What has caused the polarity within each of these components of the atom? Why is the electron negatively charged? Why is the proton positively charged? Why do neutrons have no charge? What is the nucleus of the atom? You must recognize that electrons, protons and neutrons are indeed higher derivatives of 'Information'. The electron takes its form on the basis of an 'Information Code' that assimilates and yields an application of a specific number of electrons having a specific amount of energy. Therefore, each electron takes its form from an 'Information Code' that is not very different than the Genetic Code. The form and identity of this 'Information Code' boils down to low-level Pulses as they do in sub-genes. The same is true for protons and neutrons. Then, the nucleus represents an 'Information' basis that 'Balances' all the interacting charges and energies. This 'Balance' assimilates the combined 'Information Codes' within each aspect of the atom, and applies itself in the form of Mass. The identification of atomic numbers in the Periodic Table are actually 'Information Codes' that combine to yield a nucleus that has its 'Balance' on a basis of its own. This is why each substance and element is different from the other.

"Why does sodium react with chlorine to give sodium chloride? The cause of this reaction boils down to compatibility of the 'Information Codes' of the respective elements. (Your chemistry schooling stops at the level of valences.) That is why sodium does not react with mercury, for example! The 'Information Codes' are not compatible. You can compare a group of Codes to pieces of a jigsaw puzzle. Those that fit with each other form a compound. Those that don't remain as elements. Isn't that simple, Amyn?

"If you understand the fact that every atom is comprised of 'Information Codes' that boil down to different levels of 'Information Assembly and Flow', you can actually change compounds back into elements and you can alter the elements themselves. There is no such thing as an irreversible reaction! By manipulating 'Information Pulses', you can take a reaction in any direction that you desire. Hence, Amyn, if you wish to desalinate water, go down to the 'Information' level and feed the correct signals that will result in a change in the salt compound that is dissolved in the water. You can also approach this from the water angle. Earlier, We told you about cleavages in the water submolecule that can be utilized to destabilize the water molecule in order to release energy. It is 'Information Flow' and application that can be used to create these cleavages.

"You see, Chemistry boils down to 'Information'. Hence atoms, molecules and compounds do not stop at the electron, neutron and proton level. They go down to the micro level of 'Information Pulses'. If you can understand these Pulses, you can enable *a change in the formation of elements, molecules, compounds and everything. You have been revealed enough Knowledge on this subject to get your thinking process started.*

"When they say that Jesus Christ (may Peace be upon Him) walked on water, it was true! He used the 'Information Pulses' in the lowest energy levels of water to change the surface tension, which enabled Him to actually walk on the water! It was not magic! He was just more aware of these dimensions of Creation than most people around Him.

"Now you can approach energy generation and management within a context of 'Information Flow'. Understanding the basics of Chemistry at this level helps to put the pieces of the puzzle together. These are just hints from Us to the Scientists. Those that search with an open mind will discover powers that have been unknown to them. They will be able to understand chemical reactions, energy generation, energy flow, surface tension, combustion, radioactivity and all other known phenomena in Science as long as they can go down to the fundamental micro level of 'Information'.

"Now you can see why an important part of Life revolves around the acquisition, assimilation and application of Knowledge, Amyn! In Nature, everything fits together in accordance with an 'Information Baseline'. When you recognize this,

you will realize that everything you see and everything you don't see has one common Origin. You will have gained powers of Creation by reaching this stage. You will also become extremely humble because within the 'Information Baseline' you will see the Ultimate Truth. At this stage you will have recognized Your Creator. When they say that the Origin is Knowledge and Knowledge is Light, there is much truth to it. Remember, Knowledge has its basis in 'Information'. Do not confuse 'Information Flow' as being like the simple process of reading and understanding. 'Information' in Our context is the flow of very low-level Pulses that yield identity to whatever point the assimilation and application occurs. This may sound complex, but it is actually rather simple. Nature is based upon Simplicity. So are you. So is all Creation around you. Therefore the 'Information' We talk to you about is based upon total simplicity. Search deeper within this subject. When you recognize the answers, you will kick yourself for not having seen through them before! Now is as good a time as any to start your search on getting down to this fundamental level of 'Information'. Nature evolves through this 'Information' at all times. Reach out and seek out the secrets of Creation. If it is Our will, you will find the Truth."

Received on June 23, 1995.

$\mathscr{M}$ESSAGE TO THE $\mathscr{S}$CIENTIST – $\mathscr{P}$ART 5

MATHEMATICS

"Write about Mathematics! What is Mathematics? How does it work? What does it do? What can it do? The subject of Mathematics is a valuable tool that humanity has used in the Sciences and Arts. The basis for Mathematics started with the recognition of the Number Zero. Once this number had been accepted, a state of the 'Absolute' was agreed upon. From there, all numbers could emanate, on the positive, negative and all the rest of the scales that have yet been undiscovered. Algebra and geometry also emanated from these basic fundamentals of Mathematics. What has followed to date has been a series of 'manipulations' of known phenomena in

Mathematics. These manipulations, whilst useful, are limited because a set of permutations will be reached when mathematicians will be on the horizontally flattest part of an exponential curve, which is the state of diminishing returns!

"On this day, We are Revealing through you a basis for Mathematics that will yield a great expansion in the fundamental elements of Mathematics. This will place scientists and artists at the bottom of a new exponential curve, where the point or state of diminishing returns is a long ways away, if it should be allowed to exist at all!

"The Number Zero is the correct basis for Mathematics, assuming that the entire set of mathematical permutations are of a numerical order. Why does it have to be so? Can there not be other orders in Mathematics that are of a non-numerical nature, or for that matter, do not only rely on numbers? Earlier on, We said to you that the Number Zero depicted the state of the 'Absolute'. Other dimensions of Mathematics do exist or can be discovered which also rely on the state of the Absolute, but take on origins other than the numerical value of Zero.

"When you look at geometry, all your developments stop at the third dimension because three dimensions is all that the human eye can perceive. But that is no reason why Mathematics must stop at three dimensions. Take Mathematics down to the *level of the 'Information Baseline' in Nature that We told you about in the Fourth Part of Our Message to the Scientist (The Atom). When one goes down to the 'Information Baseline', one is at a state where all 'Information Pulses' of all actions and reactions throughout the Universe reach a Steady State. The process of evolution, for example, drives Creation towards this Steady State. This means that in* everything *a human being does, at all points in his or her life, lies a direct interaction with the entire Universe! Each interaction, in its own way, contributes towards this ultimate Steady State. This is the true Point of the Absolute. Why not start Mathematics from here? Why rely on only the Number Zero as representing the Absolute? In its own way, the Number Zero does represent the Absolute, but this is* not *the only representation of the Absolute!*

"Now consider that if you are at all times interacting with the entire Universe, then why must you stop at only three dimensions? Surely there are many, many more dimensions within the Universe! Now, expand Mathematics from the Steady State Point of the Absolute by incorporating more than three dimensions. Let us say, for the comprehension of your simple human mind, that you look mathematically as far as six dimensions. Assume for a moment that the number 6 in these six dimensions represents a vertical form of integration. Then, consider a further set of

dimensions within, say, a horizontal plane, that is non-numerical. Therefore these dimensions cannot be counted. Now take angles within the horizontal and vertical planes and let them represent additional dimensions, either numerical or non-numerical. And We tell you now, that where all these dimensions coincide is the true Point of the Absolute! This must be where Mathematics starts. Can you imagine this? Of course you cannot, because you are only thinking in three dimensions! You are only governing your imagination on the numerical basis!

"Let developments in Science go down to the 'Information' level. Let Science grasp this Knowledge. From there will emerge a New Order of Mathematics, with infinite manipulations. Wouldn't that be fascinating? Of course, you must realize that Our Creation in other Dimensions of the Universe learn all this at kindergarten! Having heard that, do you still think that the human being is the most Superior form of Creation? And if other ones of Our Creation learn these simple concepts of Mathematics of the Total Order at kindergarten, then where does the human being really fit in the pecking order? If that is easy to figure out, then where does the human being stand in front of his or her Creator? This, Our dear Amyn, is the start of the realization of True Humility. The greater the strides that Science makes in the world — "your" world (because human thinking has drawn *boundaries around its world) — the greater the Humility will be realized and inculcated in the scientists. The Scientist of All will also be the most Humble one of All. This is the Truth behind true scientific discovery."*

Received on June 24, 1995.

Message to the Scientist – Part 6

Hints to Find Information
and Limitations of Boundaries

"We give you valuable hints on how to seek and identify the micro level of 'Information Flow'. Look at a lake or a calm ocean in the midst of the bright Sun in the early afternoon. Look at the rays of the Sun as they hit each of the little ripples on the water. They make the water 'glitter'. If you look carefully, it appears as though there are millions of lights going on and off at their own respective times, with their own respective frequencies. The surface of the water, depending on the shape of the ripple, gives off a unique reflection of its own. Watch these reflections carefully. You will notice that each one is a 'Pulse' by itself. The Sunlight is reflected like a Pulse and then no trace remains of

the little flash that was given off. In fact, as you look at the water with all these Pulses of reflections, it almost looks like the water is communicating with a distant entity based upon a code of flashing lights, which We simply call glitter. 'Information' flows in a similar way. There are low-level energy Pulses that are carried within the channel of 'Information Flow'. Whilst each Pulse travels, there is no trace left behind of its existence, except within the Code, where a form of imprint remains. This Code, as We told you earlier, can be called the 'Information Code', Genetic Code, Submolecular Code, or whatever else you may choose to call it. Measuring and detecting devices for these Pulses will be invented in time to come. These devices will have to be capable of 'hearing' what travels within these Pulses. Therefore, there must be no interference within and around the device because a small level of interference can drown the signal(s) that are being sought. When a human being meditates, We have said in earlier Chapters that the mind must be totally silent. Only then can he or she 'hear' the Inner Self. The identification of 'Information Flow' follows the same set of rules. When We Created human beings, We bestowed in each being a very powerful intellect. We did the same for all Our Creation that are the human's counterparts in the Universe. These counterparts are more — far more — advanced than humans, despite the fact that an equal intellectual capacity has been granted to all.

Humanity's backwardness stems from a lack of 'awareness' of the interactions that occur within the human being and his or her environment. Humans have stayed at the macro level and failed to reach the level of 'Information Assembly and Flow'. This is because they have 'restricted' themselves from true growth in their intellect and awareness.

"The classic human failing is the intense desire to draw Boundaries around everything. The Laws of Science, for example, as stipulated by humans, have severely limited the extent to which humanity can make deep and meaningful discoveries of Knowledge. The Sociological aspects of human beings are such that they only feel secure when they have drawn a boundary around themselves. Look at when We created the world! We never placed borders and Boundaries between nations and people. These Boundaries limited the human race to a culture and a society of its own. How could human beings possibly grow within such tight confines? From the time that a child is born, it is so quickly conditioned into drawing security through building Boundaries that it stands no chance of discovering Real Knowledge which demands total Flexibility and Openness of the mind! The weakness of selfishness also comes from the boundary building. Human beings like to take the most that they can and place it within their boundary in order to feel secure. The selfishness closes the mind to greater Realities. This selfishness is followed by greed.

"Greed conditions human actions to their severe detriment because you must remember that every action of every member of the Creation has a distinct interaction with the Universe. This greed draws interactions that stifle intellectual growth and awareness. After greed comes pride, for he or she that has accumulated more than others feels powerful. Pride is the opposite of humility, and True Humility is essential for discovery of the Truth. Therefore, the natural reaction to pride within the interaction of the Universe is to close the doors of True Knowledge to humanity. After pride and power comes the human desire to impose their will on others by ruling upon them. This yields to human beings an illusion of power and authority. In the Universe and in all Creation, there is only one authority and that is the Origin of All Things. Therefore, the natural reaction within the Universe towards false exercise or possession of authority is to yield an environment that counters or destroys this authority. In this way, you can examine most of the traits of humanity. It will become abundantly clear to you as to why human beings are not as advanced as their counterparts in the Universe.

"Even the whole concept behind the creation of an economy and the imbalance in distribution of resources in the world as a result of the economic Boundaries, has taken humanity much further away from becoming aware of the Truth and the Knowledge of the Universe. The Boundaries that humans have built around economies have fuelled

selfishness, greed, power, false authority and all other factors that are counterproductive to real progress. Look at the social structure of the human race. One man or woman feels superior to another because they place themselves in a higher class. One human feels more powerful to another because they believe that they come from a greater race, or a higher economic standing, or a combination of differentiating factors that they have imposed upon themselves and their self-created Boundaries. When humanity discovers the 'Information' level it will become abundantly clear that there is no room for Boundaries. Growth can only come from Total Flexibility. The entire social and economic fabric in this world will be dismantled, making way for the assumption of a Greater Order of Awareness. This will be followed by greater Humility, which in turn will strengthen Awareness.

"There is much for humanity to look forward to, if Our Messages and Hints are utilized properly and acted upon in a timely manner. These Messages that We have delivered through you are indeed a Mercy to humanity, for degradation of the world and Earth is occurring very rapidly. This awareness will not come through force or pressure, for that is in conflict with the Universe. Therefore if people choose not to heed this Message, you need say or do no more, for you will have fulfilled your role as a Messenger. The only way in which awareness will grow is if a true thirst and yearning for the Knowledge of the Universe comes about within

humanity. In the absence of this humble desire, nothing of substance can be discovered.

"There will be many that will stop to think about this Message. Some will go down to look at the glitter in the lakes and Oceans. Some will dig deeper into the Pulses that are revealed by the glitter. Then, one day, a human being will identify the level of 'Information'. After that will come about a rapid change in humanity and the future of the planet Earth.

"Never before have We directly revealed so much Knowledge about Science at such a depth. You have been given a lot to ponder upon. Break all your Boundaries and start your search. Be humble and become Still within yourself. In the midst of this Calm and Stillness, you will 'hear' the 'Information' and Knowledge. Your search will extend deeper and so will your discoveries. Remember, at one time We told you that there are twelve dimensions to Science. Humanity is scratching the surface of the first dimension. By applying this Revelation carefully, a multitude of dimensions of Science will be disclosed to you. In the midst of all this, you must always remain in close touch with your Inner Self. You must indeed pay great attention to all your 'feelings' for they too originate from the 'Information' level. The Boundaries of human beings often crush the true life of 'feelings'. Therein, growth is severely inhibited.

"Allow Love to permeate you and all those around you. This will heighten your awareness for that is a natural reaction of the Universe. So, draw as much as you can from true Love. This Love can be for another human being, or for Art or Science, or exploring, or whatever you may do for that matter. This Love will grow within you and will emanate from you towards all Creation. Then you will know that you are treading along the right path. Remember that no human being can tell you what the right path is. Even clergymen or priests, who often claim to have Knowledge of the right path, are indeed a long ways away from it. The right path can be approached from a religious, spiritual, physical, social and material context. Only you yourself can ascertain the right path for yourself through a deep and personal relationship between you and your Origin and hence, your Inner Self.

"We will, at Our pleasure, reveal more hints for those in Search of the Truth from time to time. Amyn, you must not lose time in spreading this Message for your duty and role is one of Our Messenger. Our blessings are with you at all times. You have nothing to fear for you are fulfilling the Commands of the Origin. May Peace be with you, Our beloved One."

Received on June 24, 1995.

$\mathscr{M}$ESSAGE TO THE $\mathscr{S}$CIENTIST – $\mathscr{P}$ART 7

TIME

"Ask them about Time. What really is Time? Do they truly *know*? How was the concept of Time created? Does a clock's ticking truly represent Time? In the world today, the constant speed of a device called the clock governs the lives of people. If a clock represents Time, then if you turn the clock back, why is it that the Events do not go back with it? As humanity was evolving, they saw the Sun rise and set each day. This is how they began to measure the day. Then, during the day, the Sun assumed different positions in the sky. Hence, this is how the day was divided up.

"Then someone invented a mechanical device that ticked at a constant speed. This speed *coincided with the position(s) of the Sun. The next thing resulted in the manufacture of a lot of these devices ticking away at the same speed. Hence the world could now measure Time. What if We were to say to you that this is indeed nonsense? If your watch ticked slightly faster than others, who are never truly synchronized, then what is to say that your Time is incorrect? Does the fact that your watch is running faster affect the Event? If not, then don't you think that synchronizing all these mechanical and electronic devices around the world to represent Time is somewhat backward? The truth is that Time is never really measurable in physical terms. Your attempt to use a device, which someone from outer space could mistake for a toy with hands that move, is not truly appropriate for measuring Time. Go back to the fundamentals. Assume that you were born in an era where this ticking toy did not exist. Does it mean that you physically do not exist in that era? Indeed you do! Does it mean that Events do not occur in that era? Indeed they do!*

"In the world of the material, in which you live, Events occur all the time around you. The best example of Time is illustrated by a river. There is a Motion that yields a Change, just like the flow of the water. This Motion goes in one direction and so does the Change. If the Motion were to stop, the river would become still and Change would cease to exist. When there is no Change, then existence comes to a standstill. Existence is very real, but in

the absence of Motion, there is no Change. What drives Motion? At the 'Information' level, the Pulses of low-level energy deliver to the 'Information Code' an instruction of Motion that causes Change to occur in a given direction. This Change in fact is the recognizable form of Time. Time, indeed, if you want to give it a definition at all, is a Rate of Change. When this rate equals zero, everything stands still. When you reverse the hands on your clock, nothing happens. However, when you reverse the Motion, then Change occurs in the opposite direction which causes Events to come back! When We say direction, the clockwise and anticlockwise phenomena are not what We are referring to, because those are features of a ticking toy. The direction is indeed the direction of Motion that is governed by the nature of the 'Information Pulses'. If Science recognizes the 'Information Level', then Time will take on a new dimension. All clocks do is to provide humanity with a basis or absolute level against which to compare the occurrence of Change. But remember, that is only a device.

"True Time really is immeasurable. As you understand Mathematics in the New Order, you will recognize why Time is immeasurable. 'Information' is the basis and Motion is the key. But Motion must not be confused with simple movement in three dimensions. This is why We gave you the example of the river as best representing Time. You see, water has far more than three dimensions. Just *because it takes the shape of its container does not mean that those are the dimensions of water. They are indeed the fixed dimensions of the container. Therefore, water flow is the best and perhaps most simplistic definition of Motion. The Change that arises from this Motion is indeed the Event. Therefore, to get a much better handle on Time, you will have to move away from toy clocks and go to the 'Information Pulses' that inscribe the Code of the Motion that yields Change. You see, rising and setting of the Sun are just observations of Change. Depending on where you are on Earth, the sunrise and sunset occur at differing moments or points in the Motion cycle. Hence, even before you reach the 'Information' level, conduct research on Motion. That will yield a better instrument to measure Change.*

"Now look at the concept of Motion and Change in your daily life. We have told you that a human being and all Our Creation is made up of two components, the Essence or Soul, and the Form. From the moment you are born, your Form is subjected to the cycle of Change through Motion, based upon 'Information'. Your Form, therefore, changes while you age. So does the Form of everything else around you Change by the same Motion. However, your Essence is NOT *subject to this Change because your Essence has its roots that are deeper than the 'Information' level itself. Your Essence has its roots within the Origin. Hence, the Soul is not governed or affected by*

Time. This is the meaning of the word 'Eternal'. It simply means that the Motion and Change that impact the Form do not have any effect on the Soul, for its roots transcend the 'Information Pulses' that govern the Code of Motion. Hence, when you die, your Form disintegrates. Since your Essence is not subject to these rules, it remains as it ever was and will be. When you die, the Change in your Form stops. Therefore, everything stands still. The energy that gave 'Life' to your Form, which is the Essence, continues because it is in a state of no Change. Your Form disintegrates and is consumed by the microbes within the Earth, until it breaks down to the elemental stage. Therefore death is simply a point where your Form ceases to be a part of the Motion and Change. Your Essence, if necessary, can take on a new Form, depending on the stage it is at in its journey. Through meditation, you can recognize the Essence, and hence the Origin. Science can go to the 'Information' level. It may even go deeper. But when the Essence is recognized, then Science — or actually, the scientist — achieves powers to create life, powers to alter Motion and Change, and so much more. But by this stage the scientist will have gained Union with the Origin and there will be no difference between him or her and the Origin.

"There have been prophecies in the world that have said that human beings will be able to control the length of their lives, not by shortening them, of course, which is rather easy, but by extending them

to unknown levels. This can be quite simple if you can understand the 'Information Code' and the 'Information Pulses'. Once you can do this, you can affect the process of evolution to balance out any changes that you generate through this 'Information'.

"Remember that in the Universe, each and every action of every Creation has its corresponding effect on the Universe. Remember the Steady State that We told you about. Well, Motion and Change are just a small factor in this equation. Yet in the world that you live in, Time is everything! We are sorry to tell you that for thirty-nine years of your life, you have been following a device that would be a toy for all it matters! Still, that is the way of your world, so you have to live within it and tell people of the much greater dimension that exists within and around them. You must spark off a scientific search in the direction that we have guided you. In some ways, Albert Einstein had started to grasp a few things and everybody followed him, but in a narrow direction.

"Remember the 'Boundaries' that We told you about? Broaden your horizons for that is how your Knowledge of Science will grow. It is amusing to watch how you are all governed by Time. Can you stop Time? Indeed yes — just stop your watch!! Whilst this may sound somewhat funny, when you grasp the level of 'Information', you will realize that

you can *stop Motion. Our Creation, who are your counterparts in the Universe, did that a long time ago; and We use the word 'time' because that is what you understand! A billion years of ticking clocks only make less than one notch in the 'Information Code'! Can you imagine the possibilities available to you when you participate in 'Information Flow'? We can't say that it's a long time away for you to get there, because Time is neither long nor short. It just cannot be measured, so don't try!*

"Share this Message with Our Creation, for they will learn from it. We love Our Creation deeply and We give them Knowledge for their betterment. So far, a lot of this Knowledge has been abused. The world was not, up to now, ready for the Knowledge that you are going to convey through Our Messages. But human intellect has reached a level where people can start to grasp what you are telling them. Peace be upon you, Our beloved Messenger."

Received on June 25, 1995.

$\mathcal{I}$N $\mathcal{S}$EARCH OF THE $\mathcal{L}$IGHT

This series of seven chapters provides special guidance for those who wish to embark upon a search for the Light of the Origin.

THIRTY-NINE

$\mathcal{I}$N $\mathcal{S}$EARCH OF THE $\mathcal{L}$IGHT – $\mathcal{P}$ART 1

MEDITATION

The search for the Light of the Origin can be a very special and enriching experience. For those who wish to embark on this wonderful process, I would recommend that a few moments be allocated each day to practice meditation.

It is not always necessary to sit in a specific position or within a specific setting in order to meditate. It is sufficient to sit or rest in a position that is most comfortable for the body, because discomfort creates distraction. The process of meditation requires focusing of the mind sharply onto one singular thought. It is very similar to tuning your radio to one channel. All background noises must be eliminated, including the noise of busy thoughts that exist within the mind!

As one prepares for meditation, it is important to try to achieve "stillness" of the body and mind. One must depart from thoughts of business, family, work and all other material events that consume the majority of our lives. One should build a sense of anticipation within oneself of the beautiful and peaceful process that is about to begin. One must become prepared to come in touch with one's very own Self!

The Revelation in this Chapter will teach us to cultivate the correct state of mind and to concentrate on a thought that will help to bring about a special inner realization within ourselves of the Light that we seek. It is important that we read this Chapter on a regular basis so that we may fully understand and digest the beautiful Keys to the Search that have been so Graciously given to us by the Origin.

I hear the Divine Voice say, *"The Universe was Created by Us to become home to all Our Creation. Each day, We Create more and more facets within the Universe. Our Creation is Continuous and has no Measure, for there is no beginning and no end. The Light of the Origin is Eternal and transcends Time for there is no beginning and no end."*

In trying to understand the wonders of Creation, we must be prepared to project our thinking to a plane that leaves our minds "open" to receive Knowledge, within a context that is so broad that it transcends time, space and matter. For this to occur, we must meditate on the *Name* of the Origin. This name can take any form, from God, to Allah, to Bhagwan, to Nature, to Origin, or to any other Name that we choose to associate with the Creator.

When we concentrate all our thoughts on This Name, it is important that a special Meaning or Key be attached to This Name. This Key will add a deeper background or dimension to the singular thought of The Name. We may select the Key that we personally wish to identify with the Name of the Origin. For example, we may think of the Origin as:

> The One who is Above Everything
>
> The One who is Eternal
>
> The One who is Continuous
>
> The One who has no Measure
>
> The One who is Infinite
>
> The One who is Absolute
>
> The One who is Nature
>
> The One who is the Creator

Many different religions ascribe qualities to the Origin. For example, in Islam, there are ninety-nine names of Allah, each one referring to a specific quality of Allah. Since the search for the Light is a very personal matter, we may select whatever meanings we wish to attach to the Name of the Origin.

When we meditate on the Name of the Origin, we are elevating our thoughts to a level that transcends this material world. Therefore, we must have *no* pre-conceived images or notions of what we may find because when the Enlightenment is received, it will be beyond all imagination.

During meditation, we must keep our minds and hearts open. There must be total humility, for we are merely a speck of dust that is seeking the Universe! What we will learn and find from the search is entirely dependent upon the Will of the Origin. We control nothing. We cannot "demand" anything for it is not our right to do so.

As we rise to the higher plane, the secrets and Knowledge of the Universe will begin to manifest within ourselves. The truth is that we all have the Knowledge of the Universe within us, for we are part of Totality. But our human mind cannot possibly perceive this Knowledge because our thoughts are normally based upon objects and events that occur on the material plane.

By rising into the higher level of consciousness, we can "open up" and receive a deep and rich recognition of the Ultimate Knowledge.

The purity of our deeds, the way we lead our lives, the way we treat others, the way we treat all Creation, and the Love that we project from within ourselves towards all Creation will all clearly influence our ability to rise to the higher plane (level of consciousness). Therefore, the search for Enlightenment is a total search. It requires purity and elevation of the body, mind and Soul. All these three aspects of ourselves must be in sync for progress to occur. Honesty that emanates from deep within our Inner Selves will ultimately open the door to this Knowledge.

I pray that we may all find Peace, Enlighten-ment and the Ultimate Knowledge. The change for Good on this Earth has begun and we can look forward to decades of immense peace and happiness. I pray that we may all be able to embark on the Search for the Light of the Origin, regardless of our races, cultures, religious beliefs or material status. Through this Search, I pray that we will realize the purpose of our lives in this world.

Today is the best time to start on this wonderful search, for the Tide of Good is in our favour and will guide us to the Shores of the Ocean of Ultimate Knowledge and Enlightenment.

Received on June 28, 1997.

FORTY

$\mathcal{I}$N $\mathcal{S}$EARCH OF THE $\mathcal{L}$IGHT — $\mathcal{P}$ART 2
LIFE: THE ILLUSION

On my fortieth birthday, I sat back and reflected on my life. I thought of my childhood and the things I had done. I smiled as I remembered my teenage years. It had been so much fun! As I reflected upon my life, I saw each year go by and experienced feelings of joy and sadness as each event passed me by. I then asked myself the questions, "Who am I?" "What am I doing here?" As I saw my life unfold before me, I realized with *certainty* that I would continue to age with time until my death. I realized that everything about my life was Temporary because with death, my material existence would end.

As I pondered over these matters, I remembered a magic show that I had seen when I was sixteen years old. The magician made things appear out of nowhere! He would pull rabbits out of a hat and split objects into smaller parts and put them back together again! I was not at all horrified when he cut through a beautiful lady with a sword and held each half of her body separately in his bare hands. I knew all this was not real and that I was simply looking at an Illusion! Everything I saw was Temporary and came to an end within a few moments. As I thought of my life and watched it unfold before me, I realized that it too was an Illusion! It was not Real! With death, the magic show of life would come to an end!

I asked myself the question, "What is Real?"

Just then, I heard the Divine Voice say, *"Amyn, that which is Real existed before the Beginning and will continue to exist after the End. Therefore, that which is Real is Eternal and has no Beginning and no End. In a human being it is only the Soul that is Real. The body and all its material surroundings are merely Illusions, for they will come and go. Everything you see in the material world is comprised of a set of highly organized physical forms that are very Temporary. They are Illusions."*

I then said, "When I look at everything around me, it seems Real because I can touch and feel all material objects."

The Divine Voice replied, *"The key answer lies in 'looking'. The two balls in your head which you call 'eyes' can only perceive the material dimension, which is an Illusion. Within an Illusion, you can touch and feel the rest of the Illusion!"*

I then asked, "How can I see the Real?"

The Divine Voice replied, *"Certainly not with your two eyes! You see, Amyn, the best way to differentiate between the Real and the Illusion is to look at yourself in a mirror. If you are Real, then the mirror will show you an image of yourself. This image is indeed an Illusion. The mirror simply Reflects your image. When you live in this world, you are living in a mirror. You see images reflected all around you, none of which are Real!*

"Every being has been blessed with a 'Third Eye', which is the Eye of the Real. Whilst you are in the mirror, if you can open your Third Eye, you will be able to 'see' the Real You that is standing before the mirror. You will be able to see your Soul."

I slowly began to understand the concept of the Real versus the Illusion. However, I needed more help. I then asked the question, "Where is my Third Eye and how do I get it to open? How can I see the Real?"

The Divine Voice replied, *"Your Third Eye is within you. It is your link to the Real. It lies in the centre of your forehead, where the spiritual energies of your being are focused. Through meditation you can search for Yourself, and in doing so, you will be searching for the Light of the Origin. By the Will of the Origin, when the veil is lifted and your Eye of the Real can 'see', you will experience Enlightenment.*

"Also, the way you lead your life is very important. If you Reflect the qualities of your Creator in every deed and action, you will be able to 'See' your Creator, The Origin."

The Divine Voice continued, *"The Origin is the Divine Core (Light) from which radiates all forms of Life. Every Soul is an extension (or Ray) of this Divine Core. Therefore, you and the Origin are indeed One. The Origin is like the Sun and your Soul is the Ray. You cannot tell them apart. Our dear Amyn, when you learn to recognize Yourself, you will have witnessed this Ray, which will lead you into the Core of the Sun."*

Received on March 2, 1994.

My dear friends, let us learn to recognize and understand that Life in this world is merely an Illusion. Let us learn to place less importance on material possessions, which are so Temporary. Let us Reflect the attributes of the Origin in all our actions, for in doing so, we may witness the Real.

Let us pray that our Search for the Origin may lead us to Enlightenment.

FORTY-ONE

$\mathcal{I}$N $\mathcal{S}$EARCH OF THE $\mathcal{L}$IGHT – $\mathcal{P}$ART 3

THE KINGDOM OF LIGHT: THE FIVE LAWS

I looked into the brightly lit sky and heard the Divine Voice say, *"You are from the Kingdom of Light. You are Light and the Light is You."* The Holy Books say, *"God is the Light of the Heavens and the Earth."*

In all humility, I am honoured to be from the Kingdom of Light, which encompasses the Heavens, the Earth and the Universe. The Light of the Origin can be recognized by understanding the Five Laws of Source, Perfection, Uniformity, Clarity and Unity.

The Light of the Origin is the *Source* of the Kingdom of Light. As there is no difference between us and our Creator, we are the rays of Light within the Greater Light. The Origin is the Sum Total of this Light — but a Sum Total with no limits!

The Light of the Origin is *Perfect*. It is free of all the imperfections that are found in the light of the Sun (as it reaches the Earth), or the light from a local energy source, such as electricity. The Light of the Origin cannot be compared to electric light or sunlight. The word "Light" is simply used to serve as the closest approximation that can be perceived by our simple human minds.

The Light of the Origin is *Uniform* and has no intensity. Therefore, it cannot be brighter or dimmer. The Light is Uniform because it is the Light of the Source. One can never vary the Source. One can only vary what leaves the Source. This is a Statement of Universal Truth. Based upon the Laws of the Source — Perfection and Uniformity — the Light of the Origin can never be blocked by anything. Hence, there can be no shadows as the Divine Light permeates all things in all dimensions.

The Light of the Origin is *Clear*. It has no affiliations such as heat, brightness, haze, glare or reflections that can usually be found in sunlight, electrical light or any form of light that is given off with the release of energy. The Light of the Origin is Clear and Pure.

This is the most beautiful Truth about the Kingdom of Light — *Unity*. True Unity means Oneness. Light within the Greater Light that forms this Kingdom is the purest form of Unity. True Unity is non-divisible. Cut through the Light and all you will remain with is Light, once again! This is the Universal Law of *Unity*. Unlike the rainbow that has seven colours, this Light has no components. Yet within the Light of the Origin can be everything, from Knowledge, to Love, to warmth, to honesty, and Truth. But these are not components that make up the Light. Rather, it is the Light of the Origin that makes these components! The Light of the Origin can give form to anything, but nothing can give form to This Light. Therefore, everything stems from This Light. We are Light within This Greater Light. Hence, I am You and You are Me and together we are Everything. The Holy Books say, "God knows all things." Of course, by the Law of Unity, this will always be true.

It is not the human eye that can see the Light of the Origin. Rather, it is the Soul that can *recognize* its place in the Kingdom of Light and, thereby, achieve Enlightenment. It is very much like Love. The human eyes cannot see Love, but the heart can feel it. Yet the Enlightenment of the Soul goes many steps deeper because it is a phenomenon of realization rather than feeling. When you realize that you are Light within the Greater Light, you will have discovered the Origin and yourself at the same time. May you be blessed with the beautiful realization.

Received on October 12, 1994.

My dear friends, the word "Kingdom" in this Chapter should not be confused with the material definition of a territory that is governed by a King or Queen. It is simply representative of a "State of Elevation" in the spiritual context. The Light of the Origin can be recognized in this State of Elevation if we understand the five Laws: Source, Perfection, Uniformity, Clarity and Unity.

FORTY-TWO

$\mathcal{I}$N $\mathcal{S}$EARCH OF THE $\mathcal{L}$IGHT – $\mathcal{P}$ART 4
THE BALANCE OF FORM AND ESSENCE

"Knowledge is Light and Light is Knowledge. The Message that We reveal to you today is one of the most important Messages, because We are sharing with you how the Creation and the Origin are so closely fused together. We use the word 'fused' to exemplify the fact that the Creation and the Origin are indeed One.

"As you, Our Beloved Servant Amyn, have recognized, the Form and the Essence are indeed always in a state of Equilibrium. The Form pertains to the Material aspects of the Creation and the Essence pertains to the Life or Energy that is

Unseen, which governs all things in the state of the Form. When you look around you, you see the Earth, soil, grass, trees, animals, birds, insects, water, creatures of water, air, sky and all that which lies beyond Earth. Each and every form of Creation is bound together with deep inter-relationships which yield an Equilibrium of the Form. For example, you should look at food chains. On the land, you have plants that derive nutrients from the soil. These plants are consumed by herbivores, which in turn are consumed by carnivores. The smaller carnivores are consumed by the larger carnivores. When these carnivores or herbivores die, they become part of the soil and ultimately form nutrients for the plants. This is an example of a Cycle.

"The sum total of each Cycle is always Zero. The number Zero depicts the Absolute level, from which emanate other numbers. Hence all Cycles in the material form ultimately revert to the level of Equilibrium, which represents the Absolute. These Cycles in the material Form are based upon interactions between all living and non-living material elements. These Cycles also apply to the world of business, science, medicine, art and everything else. Each Cycle can only be comprised of singular aspects such as food chains or complex interacting aspects that include art, science, medicine and other similar aspects. Remember, all Forms in the material level finally reach an Equilibrium. In fact, actions in one direction cause

reactions in the other direction that lead to Equilibrium. Look at the most infamous epidemics. The scientists call it the Balance of Nature. Indeed, what they are pointing at is the Equilibrium, whose net result is Zero or the Absolute.

"Now We are going to show you how the levels of interactions are indeed connected. Imagine a still pond in which you drop a pebble. You see small ripples which are perfect circles. These ripples grow into larger ripples, which ultimately spread throughout the pond. Each level in the material Form can be viewed as a ripple or a circle. The inner circle interacts with the outer ones and vice versa. Yet, ultimately, Equilibrium is reached. At this point, the Absolute is reached. This is where rests the Essence. This is why We said to you that the Creation (Form) and the Origin (Essence) are indeed unified. All Forms emanate from the same ultimate Source, which is the Essence or the Origin.

"Even at the level of the Essence there are the same type of circles or ripples. Here, each circle is represented by a Level of Knowledge. Since Knowledge is Light, each circle is represented by Light. This is why in the Holy Books it is said that, 'Light upon Light doth God guide those that He chooses unto His Light'. In fact, the term 'Light upon Light' can be interpreted as circle of Knowledge (Light) upon circle of Knowledge (Light). Since Knowledge is common to all circles, the

gaining of Knowledge by each Soul through each lifetime brings the Soul to a level of Greater Knowledge. Finally, the Soul after many lifetimes may reach the Ultimate Knowledge, at which point it merges into Unity (or Itself). This is the state of the Absolute in the level of the Essence.

"Now you can see what the purpose of Life is. Each time your Soul takes a physical form, you live a Life where Experiences are gained daily. For those who Reflect on these Experiences, they are able to convert Experience to Knowledge. This Knowledge accumulates within the Soul as It travels from Circle of Light (Knowledge) to Circle of Light (Knowledge). Your actions, deeds, search for Knowledge and all other dimensions of your Life add to the Knowledge carried within your Soul. Each lifetime that goes by without accumulation of Light (Knowledge) is a wasted lifetime. Through one's wrong deeds, one can actually lose Knowledge and move away from the Ultimate Knowledge.

"For those that commit suicide, they have deliberately taken away the Form which helps them gain Knowledge. Hence, they come to a full standstill. They cannot take on another physical Form for they have lost their privilege to do so. They cannot advance towards the Ultimate Knowledge. They are lost eternally. Only by the Will of the Origin can that privilege be restored for a Soul that has lost its Form through suicide. In such

a case a very, very difficult journey begins all over again. Still, such Souls are more fortunate than those that are frozen in one state through suicide. Amyn, you must caution those who talk about suicide that they are talking of plunging themselves into a state of never-ending nothingness!

"Today We have revealed to you the Equilibrium that exists in the Form and in the Essence. In the Form (material) this Equilibrium reaches the Level of Absolute (Zero) wherein lies the Essence. The Equilibrium in the level of the Essence brings about Union where the Soul reaches the level of Ultimate Knowledge. The Form and Essence are hence fused together through this Equilibrium. On a spiritual level, one must search through meditation, and through one's actions reflect the characteristics of the Origin. In this way, one can rise spiritually from Light (Circle) to Light (Circle) until the Ultimate Light (Knowledge) is reached. It is possible to achieve this in one lifetime. Some Souls may take millions of lifetimes to get there. The way one leads one's Life can also take one in the reverse direction, where one can move further away from the Ultimate Light. Because of this, you must always pray to be kept firm on the Right Path.

"We have sent Our Messengers from age to age to bring Our Creation to the Right Path. They have brought with them Our Messages and this has created many religions. The time now is not for the creation of a new religion, but rather for each human being to dig deep into his or her own religion and practise it from the viewpoint of its Essence. The Essence has absolutely no relationship whatsoever with rituals and traditions. Look into the Message behind each religion after removing the clouds of rituals and traditions. You will find that all religions are equal. They carry the same Universal Message.

"At this time We must also caution humanity about the importance of respecting their Home, or their Environment. Since all elements in the material Form are closely interacting with one another, plants with animals with birds with the Ocean, etc., the Equilibrium is clearly affected by negative changes in the Environment. Through pollution trees, plants, birds, animals and all creatures on land or in water are adversely affected. This impacts on the Equilibrium and the Natural Response is to eliminate the Source of the Pollution or the Creation that causes the pollution. Remember that the Equilibrium will ALWAYS prevail. Humanity, on the other hand, won't! If humanity stops the pollution and starts to respect the Environment and all the creatures that live within it, then the Equilibrium will be gently restored. But if this does not happen, then humanity will be eliminated through self-destruction. The elimination of humanity will put an end to the negative effects on the Equilibrium and hence, the Environment. Remember, the

Equilibrium ALWAYS prevails. Call it what you will — Balance of Nature or whatever. Epidemics will come and catastrophes will follow. This will force the desired change. It is in Humanity's own hands. Stop negatively affecting the Environment through your greed and neglect, and these epidemics (and the worse things that are yet to come) will go away by themselves. If you (humanity) do not heed this warning, you will see the results as sure as day- light. This will not be the first time that humanity has been destroyed in order to restore the Balance. Many civilizations have come and gone by rising and destroying themselves. It does not have to be so for this civilization. In fact, this civilization is capable of immense progress if it leads itself in the right way. It must live in Harmony with the rest of Creation (the Environment). Remember, since Form and Essence are fused, there will be immense spiritual upliftment, Enlightenment and gain in Knowledge as humanity changes its ways to begin to live in Harmony with the Environment (Creation).

Today, Amyn, We have revealed to the world the deepest of secrets of how the Form and the Essence are connected, and how the Equilibrium exists. We have also explained to you what the purpose of Life is. And We have yielded a warning to the world to change its ways in order to enjoy a bright and happy future. Those that read this Chapter over and over again will find newer and deeper meanings each time they read what We have said. Peace Be Upon You."

Received on December 12, 1995.

FORTY-THREE

$\mathcal{I}$N $\mathcal{S}$EARCH OF THE $\mathcal{L}$IGHT – $\mathcal{P}$ART 5

THE ROAD TO UNIFICATION

I hear the Divine Voice say, *"When the Universe was created, it was formed from one single Unit. Within this Unit existed Knowledge, Life, Light and the Powers of Procreation. Everything started from this one Unit, and it will all end again as a single Unit. It is almost as if the powers of this Unit were dispersed and dissipated over vast areas of space, time, the dimensioned and the dimensionless, the measurable and the immeasurable, the limited and the Eternal. From One came many and from many came Infinity. Such was the course of the Universe. All life forms that were created within the Universe obeyed the same laws of dissipation and dispersion. All life forms exist within the dimensioned and the dimensionless. Every life form is limited and limitless. All life forms end up in Infinity or Eternity. Forces and energies are released and converted at each and every stage of this process. Yet the sum total of all these forces, fields and energies is Unity.*

"Can you see how simple and yet how complex the Universe is? The ultimate destiny of the Universe is to return to Unity. Hence what grew through division will come back together through assimilation and fusion. Such is the course of the Universe. Each day, all beings awake in the material plane and subject themselves to dispersion and dissipation. The net result of physical existence is an increase in the dimensions of the Universe. If each being could only stop for a moment and seek the reverse of his or her existence, he or she will begin to experience Unification. *When a being achieves Unification, then a balance is reached between the physical plane and the Eternal plane. At this point, no further dispersion occurs. A state of Equilibrium is reached. This state of Equilibrium manifests itself as Peace. Motion stops and Peace begins to engulf all aspects of the being. As one grows within the Unification, one begins to rapidly approach the Origin of the Universe. This is where one can discover the Light of the Origin."*

Received on February 11, 1996.

Let us meditate on the Revelation which says, *"If each being could only stop for a moment and seek the reverse of his or her existence, he or she will begin to experience Unification."* This is a wonderful means by which we can search for the Light. Everything in our life is based upon ever-increasing material elements. Everything divides and multiplies itself, just like the process of fission in atoms. However, if we can start to reverse this process in our meditation, everything that was divided will start to come *together* until Unity is reached. This is synonymous with the process of fusion in atoms. When true Unity is experienced, the Light of the Origin will become "visible." For this we must always strive.

This Message can be understood in many different ways, ranging from the purely Spiritual to the totally material. Let us search for as many meanings as we can find in this Message.

FORTY-FOUR

In Search of the Light – Part 6

the Ray

*"That which is hidden is more visible
than that which is not."*

I am sitting in the lounge at Narita Airport in Tokyo,
looking out of a huge glass window at the sky. It is
around 4:00 o'clock in the afternoon. I see the Sun; it is
bright, but I can still look at it without being dazzled.
Then comes a cloud that hides the Sun from my eyes. But
before the Sun disappears, I hear the Divine Voice say,
"Look! What do you see? Amyn, look!" I can no
longer see the Sun; but I can see a hundred brilliant rays,
like perfect straight lines, break through the clouds and
reach out to the Earth. A moment ago, these rays were
invisible because I could see the Sun itself. Now that the

Sun is hidden, the rays become clear! Then the Voice says to me, *"That which is hidden is more visible than that which is not."* These words keep repeating themselves to me. In a way, they are contradictory in the context of this material world. In the first place, how can what is hidden be visible at all? Yet I am told that what is hidden is *more* visible than what is not hidden. In this beautiful Statement lies the answer to a deep, mystical mystery. Meditate on it, and you may find the answer.

There are so many meanings to this Statement. Take for example a young lady. You can see her physical form. What does it tell you? Nothing! Maybe she is pretty, or maybe not. Maybe she is tall, or maybe not. Maybe many things — and then, maybe not! But if she radiates Love, care, honesty, sincerity and feelings of peace, she is more visible to me! Yet Love, care, honesty, sincerity and peace are hidden. They have no visible form. However their presence makes a being truly visible!

Received on September 23, 1994.

Let us concentrate within ourselves to seek the unseen elements that reside within us. Let us think about them, feel them, and then share them; for we will radiate with a clarity that we have never known before. We may not be able to see

ourselves radiate, for these are qualities of the "hidden." To those around us, these qualities will be most visible.

Let us seek with sincerity, in the inner depths of our being, for that which is hidden. For when we seek in honesty, it will become visible to us by the Will of the Origin; for after all, **"That which is hidden is more visible than that which is not."**

The eyes of this world, which are the eyes of the Illusion, cannot see the "hidden." Let us Strive to develop our Inner Visions, which represent the Eyes of the "Real," so that we may be able to see the "hidden."

FORTY-FIVE

IN SEARCH OF THE LIGHT – PART 7

THE SECRET OF LIFE

The night is on its slow journey through shades and shades of darkness. The time is 3:00 a.m. and I am in deep sleep. I feel so cozy in my warm bed. At this point, every limb of my body is in deep sleep. In my mind flash pictures of events and places that I am either imagining or I may have actually visited. In the midst of these pictures I hear the Divine Voice say, *"Awake in the Name of the Origin."* This makes me want to pull my blanket over my head and sink into deeper sleep.

I hear the sound of a droplet of water that keeps falling over and over again onto the clear silver surface of a pond. The noise gets louder. The precision and regularity with which the droplet keeps bouncing itself onto the pond begins to irritate me. What on Earth is this wretched noise? I say to myself. I can now begin to see this droplet. It falls onto the pond and then bounces right up again, and then falls back again, and so on. What is most strange is that this droplet never merges into the pond. It is a droplet of water with an identity of its own. And yet, one would expect the droplet to disappear into the pond.

Then the Divine Voice calls out to me again and says, *"Awake in the Name of the Origin."* I am so sleepy that all this just seems to be like a dream. Then I see the droplet and the pond again. But now many droplets have started to fall onto the pond, and yet, none of them merge into the silver-coloured water. The strange thing is that these droplets never cease to keep bouncing off the pond surface. They never stop. They cannot be still. There are no clouds in the sky and there is just enough light from the stars to help me see what is going on with these droplets. At 3:00 a.m. it is extremely difficult to do anything but to cuddle up into my blanket and sleep.

Again I am commanded to awake by the Divine Voice. For some reason, my entire body feels like it is made of lead. I cannot move. The picture of the pond and the droplets continues to dwell in my mind. Then, from the midst of the dark sky beams down a powerful ray of Light onto the pond. Now the colour of the pond is golden. I can now see each droplet fall onto the surface of the golden water. I can see each droplet begin to divide itself into many smaller droplets. No sooner has the division occurred than all the droplets return to their original size. I am now starting to awake. The beam of

Light now changes from its single ray into a widespread umbrella of Light. The darkness is gone. All that stands in front of me is Light. I wake up with a start and sit up in my bed. The room is pitch dark. I am confused with everything that has gone on in my sleep.

All of a sudden, I hear the Divine Voice say to me, *"At last you are awake, Amyn. I Commanded you three times to wake up, but you chose to keep sleeping. I showed you one drop bouncing on the pond as a sign for you to learn from. Your mind was so sleepy that you never stopped to ask yourself as to why this one droplet kept bouncing over the pond, with precise continuity. And why was it that the droplet never merged into the water? But you did not understand the sign that stared you in the eyes.*

"Then I summoned you to awake again, but to no avail. Therefore I showed you the next sign of many droplets bouncing off the surface of the pond. From a single, simple droplet which gave you such a clear picture, you now had to look at thousands of droplets falling. Therefore, the picture was no longer as clear as before. After all, you had lost your first chance to figure out the 'Secret of Life' through that one droplet. Now, Amyn, you had a second chance with a picture that was more difficult. But still you never got the Message. You failed to understand. You never asked the questions, 'Why are so many droplets bouncing off the pond surface with such regularity? Why don't they merge into the pond water? Why don't they merge into one

another? Why don't they bounce off each other? These are indeed important questions that need to be asked to receive the Knowledge behind the 'Secret of Life'.

"After giving you two chances, I could have left you alone and you would never have remembered a thing! You may have had a small glimpse of a strange dream in the morning, but you would remember nothing!

"Remember, my dear Amyn, I love you deeply for you are My Creation. Therefore I gave you a third chance. This time, I sent a Ray of My Light from the Heavens into the picture that you were looking at. This Ray showed you the thousands of droplets bouncing off the surface of the pond, which was now golden in colour. The Ray also showed you droplets dividing themselves into more droplets as they bounced off the pond. You never stopped to ask the questions, 'Where did the Ray of Light come from? What is it doing in this picture? Why are the droplets dividing themselves? Why are they all returning to their original size as soon as they have divided themselves?' And, of course, 'Why are none of the droplets merging with one another or merging into the golden pond?' This was the third vision I gave you of the 'Secret of Life'.

"Each of these three visions was so important. If you had seen through the first vision you would not have needed to see the next vision because you would have grasped the 'Secret of Life'. After your

REFLECTIONS from the ORIGIN

second vision I had to show you the third vision with the power of My Light, for you still had not grasped the Mystical Message that was being given to you. You must meditate deeply on these three visions if you wish to know the 'Secret of Life'.

"You must start with the simplest vision first. Then you must understand the fundamental differences between each of the three visions. If you can grasp this Message, you will have received the Knowledge of the Universe in a multitude of its dimensions. The last vision before you fully awoke was My Divine Light spreading from one single Ray into an Umbrella of Light. That, Amyn, is My Mercy upon you. For, if I had chosen to, I could have let the curtain of darkness fall over your eyes after the third vision for you had not obeyed My Commands. You would have let the most precious gems of Knowledge slip through your fingers as a result of your sleep and laziness. But, My Beloved One, I showered you with My Love by awakening you with the Umbrella of Light.

"Your room was pitch dark. The eyes in your head could only see this darkness. Yet the Eyes of your Inner Self continued to see the Light. This is My Sign to you that there is Hope. Share this Mystical Message with others and encourage them to search for the True Meaning behind these three visions. The fortunate ones will see through it right away. Others will require more time, meditation and thought. And then there will be others that will be

too lazy to pursue the search for the 'Secret of Life', just like you were in your sleep!

"Remember that your body needs its rest through sleep. And yet, some of the most precious gems of Knowledge pass you by as you sleep and you never even knew that they had tenderly knocked on your door! Remember, it was 3:00 a.m. when I called on you to awake. This is the hour of deepest sleep for most human beings. Yet this is also the hour when the greatest Knowledge comes to you. Remember, anything of value does not come easily. You have to battle with your mind to let you wake up at these 'small hours of the night', for these are hours of the 'greatest spiritual profit' to you. The choice is yours.

"Through My Mercy, I have granted you the inspiration to write about the 'Secret of Life' for all those who care to benefit from it. Grasp onto this Mystical Message and do yourself the favour of waking up for meditation in the small hours of the night. There is a lot more to come to you. You are like a dry oasis in the desert. Open yourself up to the heavy cloud that stands above you, for you may receive rainfall in abundance!"

Received on April 14, 1995.

FORTY-SIX

*T*HE 66 *S*TEPS:

MY ASCENSION TO THE LIGHT

I walked down the streets of the old city in Jerusalem, watching little children play at the doorsteps of their homes. The buildings were several hundreds of years old. The narrow streets allowed for only pedestrian traffic and possibly horsecarts. After walking a long distance I stopped at a building whose facade was almost greyish-black from age. At the door the written numbers had faded; the wood of the door was black with age. A rusted metal ring hung in the centre, which I presumed at some time had been used by visitors to announce their presence. Cobwebs hung from the sides of the door-frame. It seemed as though no one had entered this building in centuries! I felt a strange sense of familiarity about this place. Perhaps I had been here before. There was suddenly a deep silence in the atmosphere and the more I looked at this building, the greater my nostalgia grew. What is it about this place? I asked myself.

I gently pushed at the door, and to my surprise, it creaked open! I could have sworn that it had looked bolted shut. I pushed the door wide open and looked into this mysterious building. Ahead of me was a staircase that seemed to go on forever! The steps were made of stone that showed the signs of their age. Each step was uneven and looked as if it had been climbed upon by millions of feet. As I looked at the steps, I saw images of these feet that had come from places far and wide. There were feet of children, of strong youths, of the middle-aged and, of course, there were feet of the aged. These feet were of people from all races of this world, black, brown, white, and all shades in between! My eyes worked their way up this staircase. It was endless! Where did it lead to? And why had all these people of great diversity tried to climb these ancient steps?

Staying put at the bottom, I carefully counted the steps. There were 66! At the 66th step, everything turned pitch dark. Something inside me kept urging me not to climb them, but to back out of this strange place and to run for my life. The eeriness made me very uncomfortable. Yet another part of me wanted to climb up these stairs to seek out the mysteries that lay ahead. I stood still in my moments of indecision.

A cool breeze began to blow by me, and I began to hear the distant sounds of a crowded marketplace. I could hear the voices of children, men, women, animals and all the lively spirits that existed in this marketplace. The sounds did not come from ahead of me, where the darkness lay. Rather the sounds seemed to be coming from within the walls that flanked this staircase. What on earth is going on here? I thought. Who are these people that I can hear, but not see?

I pulled together my courage and decided to climb this mysterious staircase. As soon as I set foot on the first step, everything went silent. I could not hear a single soul anymore! The marketplace had ceased to exist. I was not sure that I wanted to go any further! Could I ever get out of this place alive? I wondered. But then, almost by magic, my right foot lifted itself and made me climb up the next step, and my left foot the one after. I was now on the *third* step. Then I heard another strange sound that seemed to be coming from the walls. It was the sound of water, dripping from a tap into a pail of some sort. The water seemed to drip with regular frequency. Where on earth is this tap? I asked myself. I looked up the staircase and decided to count the steps again, just in case something had changed. Interestingly, from the *third* step, I could still count 66 steps ahead of me before the pitch darkness took over!

Once again, I began to climb the steps almost involuntarily. It was as if someone was guiding me up this mysterious staircase. I climbed three more steps. The sound of the dripping water had vanished! As I stood on the *sixth* step, I heard the clear ticking of a large clock that seemed to be coming through the wall! It must have been a huge grandfather clock. It ticked away with amazing precision.

I then climbed three more steps to the *ninth* step. The clock had stopped ticking, but now I could hear the beautiful sound of children frolicking in a playfield. They laughed and yelled as they joyfully played a game that I could not quite recognize. There must have been 10 to 15 children. I counted the steps that lay ahead of me and still there continued to be 66 steps between me and the darkness.

As I climbed up three more steps to the *twelfth* step, the voices of the children in the playfield disappeared. I was now getting used to the sudden changes in audio-scenery! On the twelfth step, I heard the refreshing sound of a waterfall. I was standing in the middle of a hundred-foot waterfall which I could not see! And still, ahead of me lay 66 steps.

I looked behind me and was amazed to see that the darkness had formed a wall! I could not even see one step back. I was trapped by darkness which now existed behind me and at the dark curtain that stood ahead of me, 66 steps away. At all times, there were 66 steps that lay between me and the darkness. However, I was no longer afraid. Rather, I was quite curious to find out the mystery behind this unusual staircase. Of course, I could not tell if it was a 66-step staircase or a 166-step staircase. This staircase could have been infinite!

I took three more steps to the *fifteenth* step. As expected, the waterfall ceased to exist. On the fifteenth step, I heard the sounds of a temple with monks praying.

They sang their prayer in soft humming voices. I could hear them all around me, but I could see nothing. I could not understand the words that they uttered as they prayed. A quick count told me once again that there were exactly 66 steps ahead of me.

I then climbed three more steps to the *eighteenth* step. The sound of the monks had died down, but I could now hear the sounds of the wind as it gently rattled the leaves of palm trees near the Ocean. I imagined a gorgeous beach with pure white sand, with a wall of these gentle palm trees standing between the beach and the mainland.

I climbed up three more steps to the *twenty-first* step. The palm trees vanished and I could now hear music from one of the finest orchestras I have ever heard. I do not think that such an orchestra could ever exist on this Earth. I could not recognize the tune, but I felt most comforted. I did not want this heavenly music to stop!

A few moments later, I climbed up three more steps to the *twenty-fourth* step, where I now heard the sound of the Ocean. The waves crashed against the rocks; it almost sounded as if they were trying to tell me something. What was strange was that the sounds of the orchestra had *not* stopped. I could still hear the music against the backdrop of the Ocean waves. Ahead of me still lay 66 steps!

I then climbed up three more steps to the *twenty-seventh* step. I could now hear the sound of strange creatures talking to one another. They sounded like dolphins! I could still hear the waves and the orchestra that played behind these waves! Am I under the Ocean? I asked myself.

Just then I heard the creaking sound of a door opening! Above me at the top of the staircase, the 66th step, I could see a door gently opening. Behind this door was a brilliant Light, and yet this Light only stayed behind the door; it did not illuminate the staircase! What kind of a Light is this? I asked myself. I see It ahead of me, but It does not light up anything that lies outside of the door at the 66th step! I could still hear the dolphins, the waves and the orchestra. The staircase began to tremble as the sound of thunder came from the open door.

In the midst of this thunder, I heard a powerful Voice say to me, *"Welcome to the abode of Eternity, Amyn. Climb the 66 steps that lie ahead of you and you may step into the land where everything exists in the absence of time. The steps that you have climbed thus far were the steps of time. And you have climbed twenty-seven steps thus far, Amyn. You have walked through ten Periods or Eras. The first seven Eras were distinct and had a clear break between them. The first seven Eras took you from a marketplace to a dripping tap, to the ticking clock, to children in the playfield, to the waterfall, to the monks in the temple and finally to the palm trees. What is the meaning of these seven distinct Eras? What have they tried to tell you?"*

Somewhat bewildered, I spoke out loud, "I do not know what they mean, O Light that stands behind the door."

"Think clearly, Amyn, for You must know what these seven Eras have said to you. Think in the Name of your Creator! And speak your thoughts aloud for all the Eras to hear!"

"O powerful Light with the Voice of Thunder, what if I am wrong?" I asked.

"If you visit each Era and carefully listen to everything that you have heard, you cannot possibly be wrong, Amyn," the Voice said.

"But I could not see anything in each of the seven Eras. All I could hear were sounds," I said.

"You were not meant to see anything for there was nothing to be seen, Amyn. Everything that was said to you was for you to hear. Now the time has come for You to speak about those Eras. Behold, Amyn, We are awaiting you!"

I felt a sense of calmness come over me. My mind flashed back to each Era and then I quietly spoke of what I had learned.

"O Voice of Thunder, when I walked into this building, I was all alone. There was no one with me. Outside the front door of this building was a world that I lived in. I wonder what happened to that world? But, as I looked at this staircase, I knew that this had been the path on which many Souls had trodden. The feet of all the diverse range of people that I saw told me that this staircase had been climbed by millions. Did they ever make it to the top? I know not! The marketplace that I heard in the First Era, which existed at the ground floor, was a reaffirmation that many had made this journey before me. I was not the only one. The First Era was full of life. The marketplace in this Era told me of a world that was truly material, with each person playing his or her role! It was almost like the world that I had left behind me as I entered this building. The First Era, O Voice of Thunder, was indeed a continuation of the material world that I have come from."

The Voice then said, *"Amyn, you are indeed correct. Now, what did the Second Era tell you?"*

I replied, "There was a distinct break between the First and Second Eras, for no sooner had I stepped up from the First Era, all the sounds of the marketplace ceased to exist. In the Second Era, I heard droplets of water dripping from a tap into a pail with consistent regularity. This to me was a transformation of myself from the crowds of the marketplace to the solitude of a place where only *one* event occurred, which was the dripping of the water. I had moved from the Era of Multiple Events (which was the First Era) to the Era of a Singular Event. My focus had gone from a broad level down to a narrow level. The significance of the water was the fact that water is the common element in all life forms, from humans to birds to animals to plants, to forests, to rivers, to Oceans to Everything. Hence my focus had narrowed to the slow dripping flow of the 'Essence of Life', which is the water."

The Voice then said, *"Amyn, you are correct. We are glad to see that you not only recognized the sharpening of your focus, but you also saw through the water as being the Essence of Life. Therefore, your focus had narrowed down to one of the fundamental ingredients of Life. But at this stage, Amyn, everything is still at a material plane."*

I quietly replied, "That is indeed true, O Voice of Thunder." I then said, "The Third Era was a further transformation from the *seen* to the *unseen*. My focus in the Second Era had narrowed down to water, the Essence of Life. Yet, this is water that I can see in physical terms. In the Third Era, the ticking of the clock was still a form of singular focus. Yet, the time that was represented by the ticking clock was from the unseen. Therefore, the Third Era took me from the plane of the seen to that of the unseen. And in the world of the material, Time is the Unseen Governor of all Events."

The Voice then replied, *"Amyn, you are indeed correct. Each Era has transformed you and you are now at the level of the Unseen. Tell us about the Fourth Era, Amyn!"*

I quietly replied, "The Fourth Era told me of the children in the playfield, which depicted a New Birth for me. I was being transformed by this New Birth into the next phase of my Being. This birth was one of joy as portrayed by the happiness of the children in the playfield. In this New Birth, I was also no longer alone, for in that playfield were many children. Hence, this New Birth was also one of companionship."

The Voice then said, *"Once Again, Amyn, you are correct. In the Fourth Era, you were reborn with joy and companionship around you. Now, tell us of the Fifth Era, Amyn."*

I quietly replied, "The Fifth Era was an Inner Enhancement of Me. The flow of the waterfall was a dimension much greater than the dripping of water from the tap in the Second Era. Water is the Essence of Life and I was now within an abundant flow of this Essence, with all its wonderful Energies. Through my New Birth, I was now granted the Essence of Life in abundance through this waterfall. Water that flows rapidly through a river and through waterfalls is Naturally Pure. Therefore, the Fifth Era also transformed me into a dimension of Purity through the cleansing by the waterfall."

The voice of thunder then said, *"Amyn, the Fifth Era is very significant, for your New Birth has taken you into Abundance of the Essence, with Purity that must always go with this Essence. You are indeed correct. Now you have moved to the Sixth Era. What has it told you?"*

I then replied, "The Sixth Era sparked within me an Inner Search for Myself. The temple signifies my body. The monks singing signifies my Inner Voice. And the fact that I can "hear" my Inner Voice is a symbol of Realization of Me. Therefore, the Sixth Era brought to me a Realization of Myself. This Era has placed me on the path of 'searching' for my Inner Self."

The Voice then said, *"Amyn, the Sixth Era is the start of a great search. This is a search that does not take you far and wide, but rather takes you deeper and deeper within yourself. You are wise in recognizing that the sound of your Inner Voice serves as a realization that there are two dimensions to you. The outer dimension, which is the Temple, is your Body. The inner dimension is your Inner Self, of which the Sixth Era has made you aware. You are now moving to the Seventh Era. Tell us about it."*

I replied, "The Seventh Era was my transition to Heaven. The palm trees and the beautiful sands depict the art of the Ultimate Creation, which resides in Heaven. The gentle rattling of the palms was a sound of Peace. The energy of the wind added a dimension of Strength to this Peace. I was being transformed in the Seventh Era to a greater order of Strength and Peace as I was led towards the beauties of Heaven."

The Voice of Thunder then said, *"Your New Birth has taken you through different stages. After recognizing your Inner Self in the Sixth Era, you have now begun to experience the Strength and Peace that reside within you in the Seventh Era. The beauty that surrounds you in this Era can only be ascribed to the Highest Order of Art as you correctly called Heaven.*

"You have learned a lot, Amyn, in these seven Eras. Now the Eras that lie ahead of you are no longer separate and distinct. They are interwoven. You have now reached the stage where you can clearly understand what they are telling you. Now you must ponder on the Eighth, Ninth, and Tenth Eras and tell us what they mean to you. Amyn, remember, once you have crossed the Seventh Era, you are no longer of the material world of finite dimensions. You have taken on a new form, which is a higher form that is not restricted by dimensions. Tell us about the Eighth Era, Amyn. And also tell us what has changed between the definite Eras and the less defined Eras. We are listening."

I quietly replied, "O Voice of Thunder, I am now undergoing a transition of infinite magnitude. At the end of the Seventh Era, I had achieved ascension to Heaven, but within distinct and separate Eras of time. I am now like a river that is beginning to merge into the Ocean. At the point when the river merges into the Ocean, there lies a phase where there is neither river, nor Ocean. If the water of the river were sweet and the Ocean were salty, and each had a separate colour of its own, then where I am as I enter the Eighth Era is the point of meeting of the river and the Ocean. At this point one cannot say that I am distinctly in the river or that I am distinctly in the Ocean. This is a phase of transition. This is why the next three Eras are not separate and distinct. Each one carries over into the other. This, O Voice of

Thunder, is the transitionary phase of three Eras that will lead me into the Ultimate Truth."

The Voice replied, *"Amyn, you have now ascended to a level of Knowledge that will lead you to the Origin. On Earth, We have shown signs of this transitionary phase at points where rivers meet Oceans. Some rivers flow a long ways into the Ocean and yet do not merge and become one until the 'Point of Absoluteness' is reached. In the Holy Quran, Bible and other Books of Revelations, this phase has been pointed out as a sign to Our Creation. The mystics have often wondered why a river does not instantaneously merge into the Ocean at the very point that the two meet. This, as you correctly pointed out, is the phase where the Eighth, Ninth and Tenth Eras must be experienced before the 'Point of Absoluteness' is reached. Amyn, you must now tell us of the Eighth Era; for you have now recognized the transition you are entering."*

I quietly replied, "The Eighth Era is the orchestra that plays the music of the Heavens. It is a Phase or Era of 'Harmony' for my Soul. The orchestra depicts Harmony. Every instrument is precise and yet the sound of each instrument blends harmoniously into the others to yield music that can only come from the Divine Source. In my New Birth, I have undergone transformations and have ascended to the beauties of Heaven in the Seventh Era. In the Eighth Era, all the elements of my Being are reaching a stage of Harmony with one another. And, through this

Harmony, I am experiencing Peace of the Highest Order."

The Voice then said *"Amyn, Harmony is an essential aspect of receiving the Ultimate Enlightenment, for all aspects of your being must be free of conflict. At the stage of Harmony, all conflicts are gone from within you. Could you ever imagine listening to an orchestra where the instruments are in conflict? It sounds horrible! And yet, in the world of the material, the Creation has not refined its hearing to tell the distinction between the music of conflict and that of Harmony. It is only at the Eighth Era that true Harmony is experienced within your Inner Self. Now, Amyn, you are going to the Ninth Era. Tell us what you have learned."*

In total humility, I quietly replied, "In the Ninth Era, the sounds of the Ocean signify to me an ascension to the level of Totality. The Ocean represents Totality and water in the Ocean represents the Essence of Totality. All droplets, rivers, lakes and streams ultimately enter the Ocean where they achieve Totality. In the Ninth Era, I have ascended into Totality. The distinction between Me and Totality is gone for I am now the Totality."

The Voice then said, *"Amyn, you have risen to a level in the Ninth Era where the singular identity of your Self has now merged into the Total. And Amyn, the Total is indeed the Unity. In an Ocean, all the water that has travelled from everywhere merges to form one United Ocean that can never be divisible anymore. We have now seen you merge into Unity for you are now Unity. And remember that you are still in the transitionary stage of the last three Eras. Therefore, your Harmony is merged into the Unity for all aspects of the Unity are Harmonious in nature.*

"You are now stepping into the Tenth Era, which is the final Era before the 66 steps to the Light of the Universe. What have you learned from this Era?"

I quietly and humbly replied, "The Tenth Era is the Era where I hear the creatures talking to the Ocean. They sound like dolphins, who are inhabitants of the Ocean. They represent the Voice of the Ocean. The Tenth Era, O Voice of Thunder, is the Inner Voice of Totality. When I heard my Inner Voice in the Sixth Era, it was a realization of Myself. But now I have merged into Totality and the Tenth Era is for me a Realization of the Inner Voice of Totality itself."

The Voice then said, *"Amyn, you have reached the highest level of the Ten Eras. Yes, indeed, the dolphins signify the Voice of the Ocean, just as the monks signified the Voice of the Temple. Now, the Temple for you no longer exists for you are the Ocean. Hence, the Voice of the Ocean has now become You, for You are Totality. And you are now leaving the phase of transition for you have achieved Unity, Harmony, and Realization of the Totality. Beyond the Tenth Era lie the 66 steps which will lead you through the Door of Light, where you will achieve Total Union with Us. You will then become Light yourself.*

We will now allow you to climb each of the 66 steps, one at a time. You are now in Harmony with Us and each step from here will totalize this Harmony. You are free of all conflicts. Rise and ascend, for the Door of Light awaits you."

I slowly climbed the stairs one at a time till I reached the last step before the door. The Voice then said, *"Amyn, you have climbed the 66 steps and are at the doorstep to the Light of the Universe. As you step in, by Our Command and Mercy, You have now become Us. Herein ends your journey for you have merged into the Ocean, you have reached the Point of Absoluteness. Beyond this point, you are no longer the river, but you are united into the Ocean. This is the Ocean of Light. This is the ultimate level that all Souls that We have created seek to reach. But only the ones that We bless will reach this Ocean of Light for it is solely by Our Will that this Enlightenment is achieved. From here on, you are no longer you. That is your fulfilment....*

Received on April 15, 1995.

FORTY-SEVEN

THE *C*OMMAND

"Amyn, deliver to the people My Message from East to West, North to South. Reach every corner of this Earth that you can, so that All My Creation may be reminded of Me. I am the Origin and Creator of the Heavens and the Earth. Every living thing is My Creation. Everything you see in the Universe, and all that which you do not see is My Creation. Humanity has gone astray. They have learned from My Messengers, but they have strayed away in directions they know not.

"For every Good there is always a counter-balance, that which you call bad. All I have Created is Good. All that I have bestowed is Pure. Yet, by My Will, My Creation has been granted the intellect to decide between right and wrong. I have filled every one of My Creation with Love, the deepest, *purest Love. But how this Love manifests itself is governed by intellect. The attachment of intellect to the Inner Love yields union with Me.*

"But I have also given you all a pair of eyes with which to see My Creation. Whilst these eyes can guide you in the world, they can also lead you astray. Control your eyes, that is most important. Use them for the true purpose for which I have given them to you. Do not let all that you see command your intellect, for you will go astray. That is what has happened to My Creation.

"Amyn, I command you to deliver My Words and My Mercies to all My Creation. There is no corner on this Earth that is too far for you to reach. And So You Will!"

Received on November 26, 1994.

FORTY-EIGHT

A $\mathscr{G}$LIMPSE OF $\mathscr{M}$E
A LETTER TO MY BELOVED CHILDREN
(ADIL, ALY, RAHEENA, NOORIN)

My Beloved Children,

I look out of my window and see the snowflakes gently falling onto the Earth, like a million tender cottonballs padding and soothing the soil, as if it were a sore wound. I had been in the mountains for days, all by myself. I had gone there to experience peace and silence, to be away from the noise and bustle of the city, and airports, and taxis, and hotels and restaurants! My life had been one race followed by another. I had made no time to be with myself. When I reflect about what has happened to me, I wonder whether I have failed to pick up the true richness of life.

I was born in a small town in Tanzania, called Arusha, which lies at the foot of Mount Kilimanjaro. The first two years of my life were spent on a farm in a tiny village outside of Arusha. Later, my parents (your grandparents) moved to the coastal town of Mombasa in Kenya, where I grew up and completed my high school education. I went to boarding school in England and then did a degree in Chemical Engineering at Aston University in Birmingham, U.K. What is ironic is that Chemical Engineering was the last thing on my mind throughout my school years. I had always wanted to become a neurosurgeon, and took all the courses that led me towards the field of medicine. Yet no medical schools were willing to offer me a place prior to completion of my A Level exams. And then, at the insistence of my brother, your Uncle Wally, who was a production engineering student at the time, I went to visit Aston University and took an interview in Chemical Engineering. I was accepted on the spot, despite the fact that I had not taken mathematics at A Level. Yet when I graduated from Aston I passed with First Class Honours, which goes to show that you can achieve anything you want providing you set your mind, heart and desires to it!

I then joined the Davy McKee organization, one of the world's largest engineering companies, where I worked on the development of mineral processing projects worldwide. My career with Davy took me to Canada, where I met your mother (Karima), got married to her, and settled down to having a family.

In 1987, I left Davy to start my own company, Casmyn. I travelled to India for the first time shortly after starting Casmyn. My initial reaction to India was one of shock and sadness. India represents my roots, for my great-grandfather, Dahya Lalji, was actually the Diwan or Governor of Porbunder State. He was a teacher of the great Mahatma Gandhi. And yet, my first ever visit to India was so traumatic! I saw children barely able to cry because they were so weak from malnutrition. Looking into the eyes of their mothers told me what the true meaning of the word "helpless" was. How could I have grown up in a society with so much material wellbeing when through each moment of my existence there were children dying of disease and starvation on the other side of the Earth! How could I ever relax and enjoy my North American surroundings any more, knowing well that so much needed to be done for the people in India, or all the developing nations, for that matter!

During that trip in 1987 I made a promise to the children that I saw that *I would be back for them*. I made a promise to all the needy children of this world that I would dedicate my life towards their upliftment. But I am only one man! How can I ever achieve these goals by myself? When you dedicate your life and energies for the betterment of humanity, God is with you. Therefore, you are now in the majority. Even if you were alone in an auditorium with a hundred thousand strangers around you, you would still always be in the majority! From that day on, my life took a drastic turn.

My engineering practice in Casmyn grew and prospered until the 1990/91 recession in Canada took its toll. We moved our office and laboratories to Reno, Nevada, U.S.A., where a large number of our clients were headquartered. Nevada is at the heart of the U.S. mining industry. In Reno we prospered further and went into developing our own projects rather than being consultants to others. Through the handling of toxic effluent wastes from mineral processing and testing operations we developed the Diamond Rain water-purification technology. It is capable of purifying water from rivers, lakes, boreholes, and municipal sources, hence producing safe, chemical-free and germ-free water for drinking. My intention had always been to help improve the quality of life of people in the developing world. My goal was to reduce infant mortality through the provision of primary care to children. What better way to start than by providing them with safe drinking water, thus eliminating contraction of diseases such as cholera, typhoid, dysentery, etc.! All of a sudden, I was blessed with an integral tool to fulfil my purpose. But technology and goodwill alone are never sufficient. One needs financial resources to enable sustainable development in these communities.

Our companies began to trade on the public stock exchange. This is where we raised some of our initial capital. My entry into the public stock market was also a horrific experience since I walked into the arena with no expertise and quickly got taken to the cleaners by the sharks! Thank God, all I lost was my clothes, but not my body! I slowly learned the rules of the game, surrounded by people with many years of experience in public markets. Indeed, during my initiation to the stock markets I did make a lot of mistakes. I was naive and trusting, which is a losing combination in this day and age! As we began to grow, I was able to cultivate strategic and important relationships with the leaders of developing nations, including countries such as Vietnam, Ghana, the Southern African nations, etc. Although our water-purification technology was a world-class solution to the critical global problem, our financial history was always stormy since we were a young company entering a huge global arena. Not an easy task, my Beloved Children!

But, God and Mother Nature have their ways! Our minerals division had been actively working in Southern Africa in pursuit of precious stones, base metals and gold. Over time, we recognized that we could be holding the mineral rights on a world-class gold deposit. And, if we were successful, we would now have our own bank of assets, tenderly given to us by Mother Earth, so that we may use this wealth to improve the lives of millions around the globe! Of course, these noble objectives can only be met in a businesslike fashion, that generates returns for shareholders.

My dear Children, think about it! In 1987 I took a vow to dedicate my life to improving the lives of others, children in particular. I gave up precious time with my children and wife, travelled all over the world, put deals together and pounded the pavement in search of funding for our companies. It was no easy task. No sum of money could ever satisfy the efforts that I have put into these companies. The efforts and sacrifices of your mother, Karima, who lived like a widow because I was always away, and the four of you, who only had the occasional privilege of being with your father, can only be accounted for under the category of "Priceless." There is no monetary value that can be ascribed towards the mission that we have undertaken together.

My dear Children, life has taught me many lessons, which I wish to share with you in the form of the following advice:

1. *Always take a hard look at all the events in your life that have gone by. Look at where I started my life, and now, look at where I have come to. **The past is a barometer that helps guide the future.** Before undertaking a plan for the future, consult your mental database of the past, for in <u>all</u> cases, you will find invaluable advice and direction towards the future.*

2. ***Always have a primary goal in your life,** which is then surrounded by secondary and tertiary goals. This primary goal must be "internalized," i.e., it must permeate from your mind into your heart, Soul and your total being. Your primary goal must become an integral part of you. It is my primary goal of helping children all over the world that has shaped the path I am treading on today. When I set that goal, I did not know that I would be blessed with tools like the water technology, broader intellectual and business dimensions, flexibility to fit into multiple cultures from a business and social perspective, wealth to fund our mission, and so on! You see, my goal became Me and I am part of Mother Earth. So I received*

all the tools, including immense resources that Mother Earth opened her purses to me for. How could a child from a little town in Tanzania become all the things that I am! In the days when I was a child, South Africa was under the apartheid system. How could I, a brown person, ever have dreamt of owning any resources in that country? You see, from my goal came a Plan, blessed by God and Nature, and success followed, with all its tribulations!

3. **You must be like a magnet, whose core is your primary goal**. *This magnet will attract good people around you, who will help in the fulfilment of your mission because unknowingly, their goals are intermeshed with yours. If your goal is to rob banks, you will attract the best criminals towards you! Remember, you are the magnet. If your goals are to do good, you will attract the best of people who will help you.*

4. **Always be humble in success and in failure**. *Look at your life to date, and you will recognize that there has been a Guiding Hand that has brought you to where you are. It is <u>not</u> you or your own virtues and strengths that have brought you this far. Hence, how can you be anything but humble, once you recognize this?!*

5. **Life is a Zero Sum Game**. *You came with nothing and you will leave with nothing. Your material possessions are not yours. You are only a custodian of these temporary possessions. What is important is how you utilize the possessions that are in your custody. If you do good with the tools that you are granted, you will take these blessings with you when you leave this world. If you misuse these tools, you will carry with you the negative implications*

that come with this misuse. This is Karma, which is very precise in its accounting. If you take yourself back to the moment you were born, then you will realize that you had no control over where your first bottle of milk would come from. You were totally helpless! I clearly remember that day! Nothing has changed today! We still control nothing, and are completely helpless. All we have learned to do is to worry about where tomorrow's bottle will come from! Therefore, live your life with faith in God and Yourself, and in total belief in your primary goal. In this way, you can <u>never</u> fail. And if you do fail, look carefully at all your actions and you will recognize that somewhere along your path, you went astray. Realign yourself and get back on course, for if your goals are unselfish and revolve around doing good, success is <u>always</u> yours.

6. **Wealth is like the Ocean. Everyone can drink from it and its level will never fall.** *But try to put the Ocean in your pocket, and you will surely drown! Keep away from greed!*

7. **Always listen to your Inner Voice.** *If a relationship, transaction, or situation does not feel right, then do <u>not</u> do it. Do not let greed or your desire for rapid gratification get in the way of your mind and your Inner Self. Remember, you are your own best friend. Respect your Inner Voice, for it can only tell you the truth. Sometimes you may not like to hear what it is telling you, so you immediately suppress it. For the moment, you may have silenced your Inner Voice, but rest assured, the problem that it was warning you against has not gone away. It is coming at you at the speed of light!*

8. *Have a firm belief in yourself.* Throughout my life, I have often found myself thinking very differently from others. For example, at University, 25 students did their computer program in one way and I did it another way. They all told me that I was wrong. One's immediate tendency would be to copy the rest of the crowd, for fear of being wrong. Yet, this is something I have never done. On this computer program, it turned out that I was right and all of them were wrong! Of course, there have been times when the reverse has occurred, too! However, by having a strong belief in yourself, you will always make your <u>own</u> decisions. If they are right, you will be saluted. If they are wrong, at least you will be blamed for <u>your</u> mistakes rather than the mistakes of others. Remember, we have come into this world alone, and we will leave alone. You and your Inner Self are inseparable. Therefore, believe in yourself, rather than follow others. Remember, sheep follow one another in a herd. But the shepherd never follows anyone but Himself (and there is no difference between God and Himself). I have always tried to be the shepherd, and not the sheep. Of course, this comes with a price of its own, which is not always pleasant. But, it is worth it!

9. *Always see life through the eyes of others, rather than your own.* Remember that all beings around you have a "Soul" that gives them life. We are all from the same Origin and carry the same Light of our Creator in our Souls. Therefore, I am You and You are Me, and together we are Everything. Hence if I hurt you, I am hurting

myself in the process. If I love you, I am loving myself in the process. Every deed of your life must be based on this principle. I have always done business deals where the <u>first</u> question I ask myself is, "What would he or she like to get out of this deal?" The <u>second</u> question is, "What would I like to get out of this deal?" And, finally, the <u>third</u> question is, "How can I make it happen for both of us?" In every deal, there must always be two winners. There must never be any losers. I have never squeezed the last drop out of anyone, for the short-term gain has its price, which <u>will</u> have to be paid in the long run. If you find that the opposite party in a deal is too greedy and overly aggressive, do <u>not</u> do that deal.

Remember, there is a bus which stops at the bus stand every 30 minutes. *You never <u>have</u> to take the bus that does not feel right. And if you miss this one, the next one will come right along. For all you know, the next one may be far better for you than this one! I never enter a negotiation on the basis that "I <u>have</u> to do this deal." I always start with the premise, "I do <u>not have</u> to do this deal." And from there on, things go in a way that is best for you because you do not force anything. Now you are thinking in the same mode as Nature. Nothing in Nature is done by force. Plants and trees are never forced to grow — they take their time. The Sun rises and sets when the time is right. Nature follows the Law of Evolution and not Intervention. Hence, what I am saying, my dear Children, is let your life evolve. Do not intervene in it. This must apply to yourself, your relationships with others, your attitude towards your loved ones, your style in business and society, and everything about you. Therefore, when you are* able to see the world through the eyes of others, you are on the path of Evolution. Looking at everything through your own eyes will only force Intervention. This will create pain, grief and sorrow around you in the long run.

10. **Base your decisions and principles in life on Trust.** Trust in yourself and trust others. In the world that we live in, trust can be, and usually is, abused. But this must not take you away from trusting yourself and others. Of course, one must always be smart about how one lives one's life. Like the Holy Prophet Muhammed said, **"Trust in God, but tie your camel."** I have always found that any relationship that lacks trust is not worth having. I have been hurt many times by people that I have trusted. This has made me smarter, but I have never stopped trusting. In a strange way, I have found that trust often attracts trust. And, if everything in Nature is based upon trust, how can we be any different? When we start to become different, we become unhappy and lose our inner sense of security. Hence, with trust we came into this world and with trust we will leave. On the way, we will take the punches that come, but I know for a fact that we will never fail. That is trust.

11. **Always search for Inner Peace within yourself.** In this way, you will be at peace <u>with</u> yourself. Then you will be at peace with others. This peace must take a Higher Order. It must lead towards a search for your Inner Self. Hence this is a search for the Ultimate Truth and the Enlightenment within yourself. The achievement of this Enlightenment will create Union between you and your Creator. With this will come

immense wisdom, humility and peace. The search for
Enlightenment has been my greatest source of strength,
peace and success in my life. I have been blessed with a
closeness to the Origin, which I pray may be a blessing that
may be experienced by all beings. In my case, the search
started with daily meditation with a singular focus on the
Origin. This search then extended to every moment of my
existence for I continually "remember" the Origin, and
hence, Myself. The strength that I have derived through
this search is beyond description. One does not have to be
religious to undertake this search. Even an atheist can
meditate upon Himself, through the question, "Who am
I?" or "What is My Place in Nature?" These questions can
take any form, for that matter. But the important thing is
to "search." In this way a recognition of your Inner Self by
your intellect can be allowed to occur. For me, this search
has been a pillar of my life.

12. **Never let your desires mould the events**
around you. *Rather, let your desires follow the events.*
This principle is synonymous with the Law of Evolution
because moulding the events by your desires creates
Intervention. There are several chapters in this book that
have been dedicated to this theme. Read them carefully, my
Children.

13. **Always give freely**. *I have been blessed with the*
ability to derive joy from giving. I have constantly
experienced that the more I give, the more I receive. And
giving is not only monetary. It includes love, care,
consideration, and many other aspects of life. Remember,
Nature always gives freely. The cloud drops its rain freely.

The Sun delivers its rays freely. Everything about Nature is based upon generosity. I have found that if your hands are open, everything "flows" through you. When your hands are closed, the flow is stopped. It is like a river. The water in a flowing river is always clean. Build a dam and you will kill the river. Stagnant water smells foul. This principle has been one of my cornerstones of finding joy.

14. **Respect your body. Your body is the temple of your Soul.** *This is an aspect where I have failed, with painful consequences. I always drove myself so hard and never stopped to give my body a break. I never gave my body the exercise that it needed, either. The net result was that one illness followed another. I suffered from immense fatigue. This often hampered my progress in the fulfilment of my goals. I have learned that **your body and its energy are like a bank.** When you borrow, you must replace. When you keep taking overdrafts above and beyond what the bank can handle, something will fail, and that will be you!*

15. **Cultivate a "thick skin."** *Take criticism freely and never let anything get to you "personally," because you are a part of "Everything." My inability to take criticism caused me a lot of pain in my earlier life until I learned the hard way!*

16. **Steer clear from hatred in this world**. *There are two forces which dominate our lives. You have often played with magnets and seen these two forces in action. The first one is the force of Attraction. This draws people, animals, creatures and all of Nature together through a fundamental essence called Love. Let this Love always reside in*

you, for Attraction is the basis of Unity in Nature. The second force is what you must guard against. It is the force of "Repulsion," which manifests itself as Hate. Repulsion is in conflict with the Unity of Nature. Therefore, <u>never</u> hate anyone or anything for you belong to Unity. In your Being, there must be no room for Repulsion or Hate. Remember that each being has two aspects. The first one is the Inner Self, which is the True Identity of a Being. When I ask you, "Who are you?" will you point at your "body," or will you point at your "self"? Of course, when you die, people bury your "body" in the Earth. Does that mean that you cease to be? Of course not, for the Real You is Eternal. Therefore, you must always Love everyone around you for they are all Eternal. How can you hate anyone? The confusion arises when people fail to recognize the two aspects of a Being. The second aspect, my dear Children, is the mind or intellect. It is this mind that makes people do things that either please or displease you. Through the action of one's mind, one can inflict immense pain and grief on others. This breeds "hate" in the minds of the recipients of such inflictions. But remember, the mind also gets buried with the body into the earth when you die. Therefore, the actions of the mind are not representative of the Inner Self of each Being, which is only worthy of Love and nothing else. Hence, my dear Children, the next time you start to hate anyone for their actions, remember that there is another side to them, the Eternal side, that is only worthy of your Love. Hate is a force of destruction. You must always reflect your Creator. Creation that stems or originates from Love is harmonious with Unity. All products of hate are in a state of Repulsion that leads to destruction. Therefore, no matter how badly people may hurt you, never be so blind and weak as to allow yourself to hate them.

17. **Never be afraid to take risks.** In my life, I have taken many a risk. Remember, nothing ventured is nothing gained! If you do not cast your line in the water, I guarantee you that you will never catch the fish!

I hope and pray, my dear Children, that you will continue the mission that your mother and I have started. Of course, this mission can never be completed because it has no beginning and no end. I have shared some of the lessons with you that I have learned, which have shaped my life to date. My purpose of sharing these lessons with you is not to focus attention onto myself. Rather, I hope that my lessons can help in some small way in building a happier and more successful life for you and those that you will share these experiences with. This is my deepest and most sincere prayer for you.

All these thoughts and experiences flashed by me in the brief moment that I looked out at the snow falling on the mountain. <u>Life, my dear Children, is just like a quick snapshot. Take the right picture, for this is your chance.</u>

Your Ever Loving Dad, Amyn.

QUOTES FOR REFLECTION

I was once asked by a friend how I could measure the value of my life. To this I replied that he and I would both have to look at the world two hundred years from now.

Message to the Reader, Front Matter, page xiii.

Before I was born, I soared freely through the skies; the Beloved with the Lover. I could go wherever I wanted to go, be whatever I wanted to be, feel whatever I wanted to feel ... I was "Me."

The Gotthard Tunnel, Chapter 1, page 3.

Learn to 'Let it Be'. Do not force the events and the circumstances to meet your desires. That will make you unhappy.

The Mirage, Chapter 3, page 13.

Learn to count the blessings that you have, for they are really yours. And, do not grieve for what you do not have for they are not yours.

The Mirage, Chapter 3, page 14.

No two things can be more "equal" than you and your fellow being. Yet, no two things can be more "different" than you and your fellow being.

Essence, Chapter 4, page 17.

I am your Mother. I give you all and ask for nothing in return but your Love and Respect.

Mother Water: Her Message to the World, Chapter 5, page 19.

Why should anyone be "wrong" in their perception of God? And then, why should anyone be "right" about God? Who can judge between the right and the wrong? God only knows…!

The Sparrow and the Dove, Chapter 6, page 27.

The cactus said to the Prince: It is only the "giver" of life that has the power and right to "take" life.

The Cactus and the Prince, Chapter 7, page 36.

It is said in the Book of the Universe: "Each grain in this world has the name of he or she who is to feed from it."

Food: The Spiritual Essence of Nature, Chapter 8, page 41.

Each time we eat food, we Bond with Nature.

Food: The Spiritual Essence of Nature, Chapter 8, page 42.

Through a simple meal, a grain of rice from far away, a droplet from a cloud, a part of the Ocean, and even a ray of the Sun reaches every one of our millions of cells! Is this not a Miracle?

Food: The Spiritual Essence of Nature, Chapter 8, page 42.

Little things in life sometimes carry a large meaning. We just tend to be blind to them because of our little self-centred worlds!

The Fruit from the Blessed Tree, Chapter 10, page 50.

Marriage is the Union of two aspects of the same Soul as they are rejoined while in this world.

The Golden Ring, Chapter 11, page 53.

Allowing the mind to make decisions for the heart is like using a ten-foot metal pole instead of a paint brush to produce a painting!

The Golden Ring, Chapter 11, page 55.

In the presence of our Creator, may this Golden Ring bring both of us together in the bond that existed before our birth and that will live well beyond this Life. May we be One for Eternity.

The Golden Ring, Chapter 11, page 60.

A child is not "alive" only when it moves and kicks in the womb. This movement only reflects an evolution of its physical form.

Revelation on Pregnancy, Chapter 13, page 70.

I ask this special question of every woman: *Did your life not undergo a permanent* **change** *after the first time you made love to a man, through a union of Love?*

Revelation on Pregnancy, Chapter 13, page 71.

The woman has the very special spiritual privilege of being a mother. She is special, for the *Soul of her child is indeed a part of her very own Soul.*

Revelation on Pregnancy, Chapter 13, page 71.

Throughout the ages, humanity has always worshipped the Messenger rather than learned from the Message itself.

The New Land, Chapter 14, page 80.

There are those that are 80 years old and have not climbed the second rung of the staircase to Light. And then, there is this five-year-old who has had Union with Me. Age has nothing to do with it.

The Lost Angel, Chapter 15, page 96.

I have learned to find a great peace in myself. I have learned to be my own best friend. In this, I have found great joy. As I got to know myself, I also realized that I was not truly alone.

The Lonely Boy, Chapter 16, page 100.

A leader always belongs in a league of his own. He is different from everyone. It is indeed this difference that causes others to follow him.

The Lonely Boy, Chapter 16, page 101.

If Dawn is the start of Life, which stands on pillars of trust, then Dusk is the end of Life that must stand on pillars of accomplishment.

The Dawn, Chapter 17, page 105.

Let us lead our lives as if each day were to be our last day in this world. Let us set our priorities accordingly so that we may differentiate between what is important and what is not.

The Dawn, Chapter 17, page 106.

There can be no disappointment in life if you hold no expectations and do not cling to a desired outcome from any event.

The Horse Race: A Story of Human Nature,
Chapter 18, page 108.

When you give more than you take, you Create.

The Story of the Merchants, Chapter 19, page 117.

Human beings have to first rise like the Eagle in their Spirit and then look at the Earth as their domain. Just then, they will realize that they are greater than the Eagle, for their domain is indeed the Universe.

The Eagle, Chapter 20, page 129.

Death is the continuation of that which was interrupted by birth.

Life in this world is but a short stop in the passage of Eternity.

Death, Chapter 21, page 130.

For those of us who are parents that cling too tightly to our children, may we learn to let go, for they have a right to their own destiny. May we learn to accept that it is possible for our children to possess greater wisdom than we do.

The Loss of a Child, Chapter 22, page 143.

Children are like rosebuds, clearly shaped with rings and rings of petals that we can identify, but not see fully.

The Child in the Rose, Chapter 23, page 145.

Sadness and happiness in Life are like the Waves — one follows the other. Make the Waves your friend and you will be happy. Make them your enemy and you will be sad.

The Message of Wisdom: The Journey of Life, Chapter 24, page 152.

The Law of Karma says: Every deed or action will be met by a corresponding reaction from within the Universe.

"Now": Your Most Beautiful Moment, Chapter 25, page 156.

Life is a series of Crossroads. At each Crossroad, one has to decide whether to turn right, left or to go straight ahead or to go backwards. The selection of the direction determines what Crossroad one will face next.

"Now": Your Most Beautiful Moment, Chapter 25, page 156.

There is a very, very fine line that separates the Past and the Future, which is the Present or Now.

"Now": Your Most Beautiful Moment, Chapter 25, page 159.

When you write the word NOW backwards, it reads WON. Capture NOW and your battle will be WON!

"Now": Your Most Beautiful Moment, Chapter 25, page 161.

May we learn to recognize that the solution to abortion lies in education, at the school and family level. It is not a matter for governments and lawmakers to legislate or pass judgement upon, for the Choices and Consequences are of a very personal nature indeed.

Abortion: Choices and Consequences, Chapter 26, page 170.

The Sun said to the Earth, "The further away from Me you go, the more you will disintegrate within yourself. But, when you turn around and start coming back to Me, you will heal."

The Origin of the Earth, Chapter 27, page 176.

The Stars are not balls of fire in the sky. They are Aspects of Knowledge in the Universe.

The Stars: Aspects of Knowledge, Chapter 28, page 180.

In the Gardens of the Angels, it is said that the next thing that humanity will be able to do is to transmit Knowledge through thought itself!

The Papyrus Reed, Chapter 31, page 205.

People remind me of the fish that swim in the Ocean of water, but keep jumping out to catch little raindrops.

The Papyrus Reed, Chapter 31, page 206.

Cancer, which is the mutation of cells, is a direct result of this complex interaction and interference that humans have imposed within the process of evolution.

Message to the Scientist — Part 1, Information Flow:
Evolution, Genetics and Energy, Chapter 32, page 212.

In other parts of the Universe there are numerous intelligent life forms that are intellectually equal to or more advanced than dolphins and humans.

Message to the Scientist — Part 1, Information Flow:
Evolution, Genetics and Energy, Chapter 32, page 213.

The immune system was the target of AIDS. The nervous system is the target of the next strain to come.

Message to the Scientist — Part 1, Information Flow:
Evolution, Genetics and Energy, Chapter 32, page 214.

Humanity is going to have to learn much from its counterpart in the Ocean, the dolphin.

Message to the Scientist — Part 1, Information Flow:
Evolution, Genetics and Energy, Chapter 32, page 214.

Humanity's indulgence in genetic engineering, which is a field that they know very little about, will unleash a change that is well beyond their control.

Message to the Scientist — Part 1, Information Flow:
Evolution, Genetics and Energy, Chapter 32, page 216.

Never assume that because you cannot measure something, it does not exist.

Message to the Scientist — Part 1, Information Flow: Evolution, Genetics and Energy, Chapter 32, page 217.

The greatest single energy reservoir on Earth is water. You can have engines that use salt water as the fuel and discharge fresh water as emissions.

Message to the Scientist — Part 1, Information Flow: Evolution, Genetics and Energy, Chapter 32, page 217.

The scientist is merely an explorer who finds elements and aspects of the Creation.

Message to the Scientist — Part 2, Limitations of Scientific Laws, Chapter 33, page 221.

In Science, there are *no* Laws. If an explorer follows Laws, his or her discovery will be limited to the boundaries of what the Laws dictate.

Message to the Scientist — Part 2, Limitations of Scientific Laws, Chapter 33, page 223.

Abandon all Laws of Science and search with openness. That is the true attribute of Science — "openness and humility in the search for the Creation."

Message to the Scientist — Part 2,
Limitations of Scientific Laws, Chapter 33, page 226.

Look at dolphins. They have a sense of telepathy. They emit Information from within their brains, which is picked up by the recipients. Human beings too can exercise this sense of telepathy.

Message to the Scientist — Part 3, Discovery of New Senses:
Telepathy and Powers to Heal, Chapter 34, page 228.

One can heal oneself by pure communication internally at low energy levels.

Message to the Scientist — Part 3, Discovery of New Senses:
Telepathy and Powers to Heal, Chapter 34, page 228.

Before taking physical form, each Soul possessed ninety-nine senses. The encagement in the body reduced this to five.

Message to the Scientist — Part 3, Discovery of New Senses:
Telepathy and Powers to Heal, Chapter 34, page 229.

You can actually change compounds back into elements and you can alter the elements themselves. There is no such thing as an irreversible reaction!

Message to the Scientist — Part 4,
The Atom, Chapter 35, page 233.

When they say that Jesus Christ (may Peace be upon Him) walked on water, it was true! He used the 'Information Pulses' in the lowest energy levels of water to change the surface tension, which enabled Him to actually walk on the water!

Message to the Scientist — Part 4,
The Atom, Chapter 35, page 234.

The classic human failing is the intense desire to draw Boundaries around everything. The Laws of Science, for example, as stipulated by humans, have severely limited the extent to which humanity can make deep and meaningful discoveries of Knowledge.

Message to the Scientist — Part 6, Hints to Find Information
and Limitations of Boundaries, Chapter 37, page 243.

The Boundaries that humans have built around economies have fuelled selfishness, greed, power, false authority and all other factors that are counter-productive to real progress.

Message to the Scientist — Part 6, Hints to Find Information and Limitations of Boundaries, Chapter 37, page 244.

⁓

Remember, at one time we told you that there are twelve dimensions to Science. Humanity is scratching the surface of the first dimension.

Message to the Scientist — Part 6, Hints to Find Information and Limitations of Boundaries, Chapter 37, page 246.

⁓

Remember that no human being can tell you what the right path is. Even clergymen or priests, who often claim to have Knowledge of the right path, are indeed a long ways away from it.

Message to the Scientist — Part 6, Hints to Find Information and Limitations of Boundaries, Chapter 37, page 247.

⁓

Does a clock's ticking truly represent Time? Time indeed, if you want to give it a definition at all, is a

Rate of Change. When you reverse the Motion, then Change occurs in the opposite direction which causes Events to come back!

Message to the Scientist — Part 7,
Time, Chapter 38, page 248/50.

Death is simply a point where your Form ceases to be a part of the Motion and Change.

Message to the Scientist — Part 7,
Time, Chapter 38, page 252.

The process of meditation requires focusing of the mind sharply onto one singular thought. It is very similar to tuning your radio to one channel.

In Search of the Light — Part 1, Steps in the Search for the
Light of the Origin, Chapter 39, page 257.

Our Creation is Continuous and has no Measure, for there is no beginning and no end.

In Search of the Light — Part 1, Steps in the Search for the
Light of the Origin, Chapter 39, page 258.

Everything you see in the material world is comprised of a set of highly organized physical forms that are very Temporary. They are Illusions.

In Search of the Light — Part 2, Life:
The Illusion, Chapter 40, page 263.

Every being has been blessed with a "Third Eye," which is the Eye of the Real. It lies in the centre of your forehead, where the spiritual energies of your being are focused.

In Search of the Light — Part 2, Life:
The Illusion, Chapter 40, page 264.

The Origin is like the Sun and your Soul is the Ray. You cannot tell them apart.

In Search of the Light — Part 2, Life:
The Illusion, Chapter 40, page 265.

For those that commit suicide, they have deliberately taken away the Form which helps them gain Knowledge. Hence, they come to a full standstill. They cannot take on another physical Form for they have lost their privilege to do so. They are lost eternally.

In Search of the Light — Part 4, The Balance of
Form and Essence, Chapter 42, page 273.

We have sent Our Messengers from age to age to bring Our Creation to the Right Path. They have brought with them Our Messages and this has created many religions. The time now is not for the creation of a new religion, but rather for each human being to dig deep into his or her own religion and practice it from the viewpoint of its Essence.

In Search of the Light — Part 4, The Balance of
Form and Essence, Chapter 42, page 274.

Look into the Message behind each religion after removing the clouds of rituals and traditions. You will find that all religions are equal. They carry the same Universal Message.

In Search of the Light — Part 4, The Balance of
Form and Essence, Chapter 42, page 275.

Stop negatively affecting the Environment through your greed and neglect, and these epidemics (and the worse things that are yet to come) will go away by themselves.

In Search of the Light — Part 4, The Balance of
Form and Essence, Chapter 42, page 276.

Many civilizations have come and gone by rising and destroying themselves. It does not have to be so for this civilization. In fact, this civilization is capable of immense progress if it leads itself in the right way. It must live in Harmony with the rest of Creation (the Environment).

In Search of the Light — Part 4, The Balance of
Form and Essence, Chapter 42, page 276.

If each being could only stop for a moment and seek the reverse of his or her existence, he or she will begin to experience Unification.

In Search of the Light — Part 5,
The Road to Unification, Chapter 43, page 279.

That which is hidden is more visible than that which is not.

In Search of the Light — Part 6,
The Ray, Chapter 44, page 282.

Remember that your body needs its rest through sleep. And yet, some of the most precious gems of Knowledge pass you by as you sleep and you never even knew that they had tenderly knocked on your door!

In Search of the Light — Part 7,
The Secret of Life, Chapter 45, page 289.

From here on, you are no longer you. That is your fulfilment....

The 66 Steps: My Ascension to the Light,
Chapter 46, page 306.

I saw children barely able to cry because they were so weak from malnutrition. Looking into the eyes of their mothers told me what the true meaning of the word "helpless" was.

A Glimpse of Me: A Letter to my Beloved Children,
Chapter 48, page 311.

When you dedicate your life and energies for the betterment of humanity, God is with you. Therefore, you are now in the majority. Even if you were alone in an auditorium with a hundred thousand strangers around you, you would still always be in the majority!

A Glimpse of Me: A Letter to my Beloved Children,
Chapter 48, page 311.

The past is a barometer that helps guide the future.

A Glimpse of Me: A Letter to my Beloved Children,
Chapter 48, page 314.

Life is a Zero Sum Game.

A Glimpse of Me: A Letter to my Beloved Children,
Chapter 48, page 315.

Wealth is like the Ocean. Everyone can drink from it and its level will never fall. But try to put the Ocean in your pocket, and you will surely drown!

A Glimpse of Me: A Letter to my Beloved Children,
Chapter 48, page 316.

Always listen to your Inner Voice. If a relationship, transaction, or situation does not feel right, then do *not* do it.

A Glimpse of Me: A Letter to my Beloved Children,
Chapter 48, page 316.

Always see life through the eyes of others, rather than your own.

A Glimpse of Me: A Letter to my Beloved Children,
Chapter 48, page 317.

In every deal, there must always be two winners. There must never be any losers. I have never squeezed the last drop out of anyone, for the short-term gain has its price, which *will* have to be paid in the long run.

A Glimpse of Me: A Letter to my Beloved Children,
Chapter 48, page 318.

Base your decisions and principles in life on Trust. Trust in yourself and trust others.

A Glimpse of Me: A Letter to my Beloved Children,
Chapter 48, page 319.

Like the Holy Prophet Muhammed said, "Trust in God, but tie your camel."

A Glimpse of Me: A Letter to my Beloved Children,
Chapter 48, page 319.

Always search for Inner Peace within yourself. In this way, you will be at peace with yourself. Then, you will be at peace with others.

A Glimpse of Me: A Letter to my Beloved Children,
Chapter 48, page 319.

Respect your body. Your body is the temple of your Soul.

A Glimpse of Me: A Letter to my Beloved Children,
Chapter 48, page 321.

Your body and its energy are like a bank. When you borrow, you must replace.

A Glimpse of Me: A Letter to my Beloved Children,
Chapter 48, page 321.

Never be afraid to take risks. Remember, nothing ventured is nothing gained! If you do not cast your line in the water, I guarantee you that you will never catch the fish!

A Glimpse of Me: A Letter to my Beloved Children,
Chapter 48, page 323.

Life, my dear children, is just like a quick snapshot. Take the right picture, for this is your chance.

A Glimpse of Me: A Letter to my Beloved Children,
Chapter 48, page 323.

ORDER FORM

$\mathscr{R}$EFLECTIONS FROM THE $\mathscr{O}$RIGIN

CANADA	UNITED STATES

Hardcover Book:
___ Copies @ $32.95 $_____
Softcover book:
___ Copies @ $19.95 $_____
GST (7%) $_____
Shipping (1st book) $ 5.00
Add $3 for each
  additional book $_____
 	
Total enclosed $_____
	Hardcover Book:
	___ Copies @ $27.95 $_____
	Softcover book:
	___ Copies @ $17.95 $_____
	
	Shipping (1st book) $ 2.50
	Add $2 for each
	  additional book $_____
	
	Total enclosed $_____

Make cheque or money order payable to:

REFLECTIONS PUBLISHING

For payment by credit card:

☐ Visa   ☐ Mastercard
☐ Diners Club   ☐ American Express
☐ Interac

Card Number _____

Expiry date _____

Signature _____

Ship to:

Name _____

Address _____

_____

Phone (work) _____ (home) _____

REFLECTIONS PUBLISHING
18th Floor, 1500 West Georgia Street
Vancouver, BC Canada V6G 2Z6
In Canada and US call toll-free: 1-888-REVEAL-3
Outside Canada and US call: (604) 926-4764
Email: reflect@compuserve.com

Thank you for your order!